Aspects of the Atonement

Aspects of the Atonement

Cross and Resurrection in the Reconciling of God and Humanity

I. Howard Marshall

Paternoster:
thinking faith

LONDON ● COLORADO SPRINGS ● HYDERABAD

13 12 11 10 09 08 07   7 6 5 4 3 2 1

First published 2007 by Authentic Media
9 Holdom Avenue, Bletchley, Milton Keynes, Bucks, MK1 1QR, UK
1820 Jet Stream Drive, Colorado Springs, CO 80921, USA
OM Authentic Media, Medchal Road, Jeedimetla Village, Secunderabad
500 055, A.P., India
www.authenticmedia.co.uk
Authentic Media is a division of IBS-STL UK, a company limited by
guarantee (registered charity no. 270162)

British Library Cataloguing in Publication Data

A catalogue record for this book is available from the
British Library

ISBN-13: 978-1-84227-549-8
ISBN-10: 1-84227-549-6

Cover design by fourninezero design.
Print Management by Adare Carwin
Printed and bound in Great Britain by J.H. Haynes & Co., Sparkford

Contents

Preface

During the past few years the nature and effects of the work of Christ in his death and resurrection have become the subject of theological controversy in the UK and in North America, and I have found my attention being directed to different aspects of the problem. Various invited lectures gave me the opportunity to share my thinking on this matter.

It all started with an invitation to deliver the first of a series of lectures in memory of Professor F. F. Bruce, the distinguished Scottish New Testament scholar, at the Highland Theological College, Dingwall, on 1 October 2004; the lecture was also given as a J. E. Davey Memorial Lecture in Union Theological College, Belfast, on 30 November 2004. It was published as 'Some Thoughts on Penal Substitution' in *Irish Biblical Studies* 26:3 (2005), 119–151.

This was followed by an invitation to give a keynote address entitled 'The Theology of the Atonement' at a conference under the title 'Why did Christ die? A symposium on the theology of atonement', held under the auspices of the Evangelical Alliance at the London School of Theology, on 7 July 2004. A shortened version of the address is being published in the conference volume by Zondervan. The material in chapters 1 and 2 of this book is based on a restructuring of the material in these two papers with some revision and supplementation.

Chapter 3 is based on a Theological Society Public Lecture organised by the Chaplaincy in the University of Wales, Swansea, on 23 January 2006; it is scheduled to appear in a forthcoming volume of essays in honour of John Warwick Montgomery.

Finally, chapter 4 arises from an invitation to give a lecture on the broad topic of reconciliation in the New Testament at the biennial conference of the Fellowship of European Evangelical Theologians held in Prague on 6 August 2006.

Although the various parts of the book thus arise from different occasions, it seemed to me that there was sufficient unity between them to constitute a coherent set of essays. Between them they discuss the state of humankind from which deliverance is needed, the way in which the death of Christ functions to bring about deliverance from sin and its consequences, the (often neglected) place of the resurrection of Christ in this saving action, and the resulting offer of reconciliation with God that carries with it the obligation to bring about reconciliation among the different peoples for whom Christ died. I was, therefore, delighted to receive the invitation to deliver the Chuen King Lectures, held under the auspices of Chung Chi College, Chinese University of Hong Kong, on 24 and 26 February 2006. I was also invited to give the same series of lectures at the Seminari Theoloji Malaysia on 28 February 2006 and at the Italian Bible Institute in Rome on 12 May 2007. I am grateful to my friends in these institutions for their gracious hospitality and kind reception of my lectures.

I. Howard Marshall
May, 2007

1 The Penalty of Sin

Introduction

How are we to understand the significance of the work of Jesus Christ that is the basis of the salvation of sinners? And how are we to explain it in our presentations of the gospel to our contemporaries? These two closely related questions are probably the most important that can be put to us as biblical scholars and theologians by the church today. Karl Barth famously saw dogmatics as the service that Christian scholarship provides to the church by showing it how to be true to the gospel in its proclamation.[1] Our theme lies at the centre of our responsibility as thinking Christians.

If I have to identify myself and place myself on the theological map, there is little doubt as to where friends and critics would put me and, indeed, as to my own self-understanding. I was brought up in that area of Christianity known as evangelicalism, and I have seen no compelling reason to shift my ground over the years, although I hope that I have a better understanding of what I believe and why I should believe it than when I first began to take notice of these things. Evangelicalism is that form of the Christian faith which is associated with the revival movement that took place in Europe and North America during the eighteenth century. To say that it was a revival implies, of course, that it was not new in the sense of being different from the past, but new in

---

[1] Bromiley, G. W. "Theology as Service in Karl Barth." In Hart, T., and D. Thimell. *Christ in Our Place: The Humanity of God in Christ for the Reconciliation of the World – Essays Presented to James Torrance.* Exeter: Paternoster Press, 1991, 133–151. Barth, K. *Church Dogmatics 1:2.* Edinburgh: T & T Clark, 1956, 797–884.

the sense of being a fresh flowering of something that had died, or nearly died. Evangelical theologians would claim that they belong to a succession that stretches backwards through the Puritans, through Martin Luther and John Calvin, back to Augustine and back to the New Testament itself. For one of its characteristics, unlike its major modern rival, so-called liberalism, is that it seeks to be true to Scripture as its supreme authority in faith and doctrine, and it believes that Scripture is a faithful revelation of God and his ways.

The actual faith of evangelicals places the death of Jesus, closely associated of course with his resurrection, at the centre of its doctrine, rather than, say, the moral teaching of Jesus, and it sees as fundamental the need for individuals to make their own personal response to Jesus as Savior and Lord. In the past this has sometimes led evangelicals to a distrust of a social gospel more concerned with changing the structures of society because liberalism exalted this at the cost of playing down the importance of individual conversion.[2] More and more evangelicals, however, have come to recognize that evangelism and social action are both Christian duties. A further characteristic should be mentioned: evangelicals are people who believe that their religion and its practice are not something peripheral to daily life (as, for example, with people who attend church but rarely, and whose Christianity extends to nothing more than a vague sense of Christian principles) but should inform every part of their thought and behavior. Biblicism, crucicentrism, conversionism and activism are thus the characteristic key elements in evangelicalism, although this does not mean that other aspects of Christian faith and practice are neglected.

Central, then, in the evangelical version of Christianity is the doctrine of the work of Christ as the basis of salvation. A doctrine of the work of Christ has to deal with two aspects of the human situation: our situation as sinners in relationship to the God against whom we have sinned and our situation as

---

[2] In the UK, for example, it was people associated with liberal forms of Christianity who were least supportive of such evangelists as Billy Graham.

sinners in relation to the sin that masters us. This discussion deals primarily with the former aspect of the situation.

A traditional, and very simple, understanding of what happens in the death of Jesus Christ would be as follows. It comprises two thoughts. First, all humankind is condemned to eternal death as the penalty imposed by God for human sin. No matter how much or how little we may have sinned, there is a fixed penalty for all sinners, namely eternal death (of which physical death is both a part and a symbol).[3] Second, the death of Jesus on the cross was not merely a physical death but also the eternal death due to sinners. This death was suffered on this occasion by one who was sinless and, therefore, not because of his own sins but because of his voluntary bearing of the death that was due to other people because of their sins. His death was thus instead of their death, and consequently those who accept him as their Savior are freed from the penalty of their sins. He has died instead of them. True, they still die physically,[4] but they do not die eternally because Christ has died instead of them, and God will not require the penalty twice as it were. One can easily see how the term "penal substitution" has popularly come to be applied to this doctrine, the theological term "penal" relating to the nature of the sufferings and death of Jesus, and the term "substitution" referring to the fact that he was bearing this penalty on behalf of others and not on his own behalf.

The questions then are whether this doctrine is a correct interpretation of the New Testament teaching about the death of Christ, and in what way it can (or should) be expressed in contemporary preaching and teaching of the gospel. The discussion takes different forms in different ages and cultures,

---

[3] The "fixed penalty" is appropriate because what is ultimately being judged is not a host of individual offences of varying degrees of wickedness but rather the basic human attitude of rebellion against God and disobedience to his commands. This is not to deny that rebellion may be present to greater or lesser degree, and somehow God, in his justice, must take note of this.

[4] That is, of course, unless they survive to the second coming and are transformed as living people rather than raised from the dead.

and, in our own so-called post-modern culture, it has arisen in a particular form as the result of fresh questioning of the Christian church's traditional understanding of the gospel. During the past few years there has been much discussion within and without evangelicalism regarding the understanding of salvation "solely through the blood and righteousness of Christ."[5] So we must ask, In what way is the death of Jesus Christ the ground of our salvation?

The understanding of this death in terms of penal substitution has attracted considerable criticism from several quarters in recent years and, equally, has been upheld by its partisans. It came to the attention of the Christian public, as opposed to the academic world, through the writing of Steve Chalke who is a well-known Christian leader in the UK, a media figure, and the leader of a Trust that is very much concerned with the social witness of evangelical Christianity. With the collaboration of the freelance theologian Alan Mann, he wrote a popular book entitled *The Lost Message of Jesus*. What aroused intense discussion was not the lost elements in the message of Jesus that were brought to light, but rather the critique that was offered of elements that are usually thought to be part of that message of the earthly Jesus or of what the apostles taught about him. Turning his attention from what Jesus said to how his death was understood, Chalke explains that he believes that the spectrum of concepts that figure in a robust theology of the cross certainly includes "a clear substitutionary element." Nevertheless, he finds it most helpful to understand the cross and resurrection as victory over the forces of sin and evil that oppress people. He then goes on to say that the relatively modern idea of "penal" substitution depicts "a wrathful God who can only have his

---

[5] This understanding would be accepted by all evangelical Christians. The actual phrase is taken from the interview between the more Calvinist Charles Simeon and the more Arminian John Wesley in which their essential agreement on the fundamental doctrines of evangelicalism is established. See Moule, H. C. G. *Charles Simeon.* London: Inter-Varsity Fellowship, 1948 [originally published 1892], 79f, citing Simeon's *Horae Homileticae.* Moule opines that the interview is that recorded in Wesley's Journal for 20 December 1784.

anger at iniquitous sinners appeased through bringing about the violent death of his Son." He finds this to be incompatible with his view of the character of God in that it makes God out to be a "cosmic child abuser," whereas Jesus taught non-violence.[6] Penal substitution is held to imply that God could not save sinners until he had first exercised violence on his Son, but the unacceptability of such violence indicates that penal substitution cannot be the right way to understand the significance of the cross.[7] This then leads to attempts to show that the concept is not well-founded in Scripture, and even represents a misinterpretation of scriptural teaching.

Similarly, Alan Mann wrote: "A biblical understanding of atonement is concerned above all with the restoration of mutual, undistorted, unpolluted divine/human relationship, not with the appeasing of a God angered by the misdeeds of his creatures."[8] Both writers have subsequently drawn back somewhat from these rather forceful statements, but here we shall deal with the positions that are stated in their writings and that, in any case, could be paralleled from other sources.

In fact, such statements in popular-style writings reflect the view of a number of theologians who reject the concept of penal substitution as the principal means, or even as a subordinate means, of understanding the significance of the death of Christ. Their views would probably not have caused too much comment within the evangelical fold if they had come from those who do not claim to be evangelicals

---

[6] Chalke, S., and A. Mann. *The Lost Message of Jesus*. Grand Rapids, MI: Zondervan, 2003. The quotations above were taken from Chalke, S. "Redeeming the Cross: The Lost message of Jesus and the Cross of Christ" (internet download, courtesy of S. J. Gathercole); see also "Cross purposes." *Christianity* (September 2004), 44–48.

[7] See the discussion in Green, J. B., and M. D. Baker. *Recovering the Scandal of the Cross: Atonement in New Testament and Contemporary Contexts*. Carlisle: Paternoster Press, 2000, 30–31, 90–92.

[8] Mann, A. *Atonement for a 'Sinless' Society: Engaging with an emerging culture*. Milton Keynes: Paternoster Press, 2005, 94. It is not clear whether this statement means that a biblical understanding of atonement is not concerned *at all* with the appeasing of God or that it is not concerned *primarily* ("above all") with the appeasing of God.

in their theology. Some of them, however, do hold this doctrinal position, so their questioning of this key doctrine has caused something of a furore among those colleagues who regard penal substitution as an essential element in Christian doctrine. They include Joel Green and Mark Baker, and Stephen Travis.[9]

We should not exempt any aspect of our fundamental doctrines from theological scrutiny, since if we hold a doctrine of scriptural authority, clearly that applies only to Scripture and does not extend to human statements of Christian belief, even though we claim that they are entirely based on Scripture. We are to examine our doctrines not only to understand them correctly and express them with precision, but also to face up to any objections against them. If our doctrines are attacked, we need to explore them and see whether the criticisms are justified, frame defenses and responses, and express our doctrines in ways that will be comprehensible and meaningful to our audience.[10] In this

---

[9] Chalke, S., and A. Mann. *The Lost Message of Jesus*. Grand Rapids, MI: Zondervan, 2003; see especially Green, J. B., and M. D. Baker. *Recovering the Scandal of the Cross: Atonement in New Testament and Contemporary Contexts*. Carlisle: Paternoster Press, 2000; Goldingay, J. (ed.), *Atonement Today*. London: SPCK, 1995; Marshall, C. D. *Beyond Retribution: A New Testament Vision for Justice, Crime, and Punishment*. Grand Rapids, MI: Eerdmans, 2001; Smail, T. *Once and for all: A Confession of the Cross*. London: DLT, 1998; Travis, S. H. "Christ as Bearer of Divine Judgment in Paul's Thought about the Atonement." In Green, J. B., and M. Turner *Jesus of Nazareth Lord and Christ: Essays on the Historical Jesus and New Testament Christology*. Grand Rapids, MI: Eerdmans, 1994, 332–345, (reprinted in Goldingay, *Atonement*, 21–38).

More widely, see Bradley, I. *The Power of Sacrifice*. London: DLT, 1995; Gorringe, T. *Cross and Retribution*. Cambridge: CUP, 1996; Gunton, C. E. *The Actuality of Atonement: A Study of Metaphor, Rationality and the Christian Tradition*. Edinburgh: T & T Clark, 1988; Schwager, R. *Jesus in the Drama of Salvation: Toward a Biblical Doctrine of Redemption*. New York, NY: Crossroad, 1999; Weaver, J. D. *The Nonviolent Atonement*. Grand Rapids, MI: Eerdmans, 2001.

For a survey of recent scholarship, see McGowan, A. T. B. "Penal Substitution: J. I. Packer Revisited," paper at Tyndale Fellowship Christian Doctrine Study Group, 2004.

[10] From the traditionalist side, see Hill, C. E., and F. A. James, III (ed.). *The Glory of the Atonement: Biblical, Historical and Practical Perspectives*.

particular case, I shall argue that the doctrine is well-founded in Scripture, and that it is defensible against the objections brought against it. I hope that it may be possible to do so in such a way that, whatever may be the problems with the terminology, all of us may be able to recognize the validity and, indeed, the centrality of what is known by the term "penal substitution" instead of repudiating the concept.

What then are the problems with the doctrine of penal substitution? Here are some questions that need to be asked.

1. What is the place of penal substitution in the teaching of Scripture? There are four distinguishable views:
   • The principle of penal substitution does not figure in the New Testament at all.[11]
   • It is there, but it is only one of the pictures/metaphors/analogies used in the New Testament to express the significance of the death of Jesus Christ.[12] Some might argue that in this case it is of lesser importance or even dispensable.
   • It occurs to such an extent that it is not only indispensable but also the most important.[13]
   • It is the underlying principle present in all the others and the factor that makes them cohere.[14]

Downers Grove: IVP, 2004; Peterson, D. (ed.), *Where Wrath and Mercy Meet: Proclaiming the Atonement Today.* Carlisle: Paternoster Press, 2001.

[11] Taylor, V. *The Atonement in New Testament Teaching.* London: Epworth, 1945², 197, commented that the New Testament teaching "comes so near, without actually crossing, the bounds of substitutionary doctrine."

[12] So Gunton. *Actuality* but he does not regard it as dispensable.

[13] So Packer, J. I. "What Did the Cross Achieve? The Logic of Penal Substitution." *TynB* 25 (1974): 3–45.

[14] Peterson, D. (ed.), *Where Wrath and Mercy Meet*, 65: "all the benefits of Christ's death depend upon his sin-bearing as the innocent substitute." Cf. Stott, J. R. W. *The Cross of Christ.* Leicester: IVP, 1986, 159: "We strongly reject, therefore, every explanation of the death of Christ which does not have at its centre the principle of 'satisfaction through substitution', indeed divine self-satisfaction through divine self-substitution." Cf. Packer, J. I. "The Atonement in the Life of the Christian." In Hill and James, *Glory*, 416.

2. Is the doctrine, in fact, based on a correct understanding of the theological statements about the death of Jesus in Scripture? There is considerable debate over the nature of sacrifice, for example, whether sacrifice in the Old Testament functioned by virtue of penal substitution of the animal sacrificed for the sinner.
3. Even though it may be taught in Scripture, is it a doctrine that we can maintain today, or is it surrounded by such objections as to make it unacceptable? Here such questions arise as:
   - What is the nature of punishment? Is it retributive, or what? Bound up with this is the understanding of what is meant by guilt.
   - Is substitutionary suffering an appropriate, ethical way of saving sinners from the consequences of their sin?
4. Are there other understandings of the New Testament teaching about the death of Jesus that may be regarded as more basic than penal substitution or that may be held alongside it as parts of a total understanding of that death?
5. How are other aspects of the life and work of Jesus related to our salvation, and how do they fit in with this doctrine? In particular, how does the resurrection fit into the picture as a saving event?[15]
6. How do we present and explain the death of Christ in our preaching and evangelism today?

In this discussion I am primarily concerned with the biblical and theological foundations that underlie our preaching of the gospel and not with the evangelistic edifice that we erect on these foundations. Nevertheless, two points should be briefly noted. First, even if we were to conclude that it is not helpful to use terms like "penal suffering" or "appeasing God" in our preaching, we still need to ask whether there is a place for them and what is meant by them in our technical theology. Second, we cannot evade the problem of how we communicate biblical theology to unbelievers with a different

---

[15] This topic is taken up separately in Chapter 3.

world-view from ours. Here I warmly appreciate the work done by various evangelical authors in trying to find new ways of expressing the significance of the cross for people today. I regret that my appreciation may be obscured by the need to concentrate in my limited treatment on what they have to say about the traditional understanding of the cross and to do so in critical mode.

All of this combines to make an agenda far greater than can be addressed in the space at my disposal. I can do no more than introduce some of these questions and give some pointers that I hope may help us to answer them. In particular, I cannot take up the final question of how we convey the message of the cross in our evangelistic preaching.

Some basic affirmations

Let me begin by stating some basic truths that I consider to be essential to a New Testament theology of salvation.

1. We are saved from the consequences of our sins by the grace of God and not by anything that we ourselves can do.
2. In the death of Jesus, the Father and the Son are acting together in love, so that there is no question that the Son was acting to persuade an otherwise unwilling Father to forgive; the source of the atonement lies in the gracious agreement of Father and Son.
3. The decisive element in our salvation is the death of Jesus, or rather, the death and the resurrection of Jesus. "Christ died for us" (Rom. 5:8) and "Christ died for our sins" (1 Cor. 15:3) are fundamental Christian confessions as is he "was delivered over to death for our sins and was raised to life for our justification" (Rom. 4:25).
4. This death is the death of one who is, at one and the same time, the Son of God and the sinless human being, the second Adam.

5. It follows that the incarnation was an essential condition for the saving action.
6. The salvation secured by the death and resurrection of Jesus becomes effective through the work of the Holy Spirit and through the faith of the recipient.
7. The main results of the atonement are, negatively, to deliver us from the guilt and power of sin and, positively, to restore us to a right relationship with God with all that that involves.

Any doctrine of the death of Jesus must conform to or incorporate these basic points, which are clearly taught in the New Testament. They would surely be upheld by theologians generally, whether or not they are comfortable with the doctrine expressed by the term "penal substitution." However, this basic core of belief leaves unanswered just how the death of Jesus is the means of salvation.

The use of metaphor

An important preliminary point is the acknowledged fact that the New Testament uses various forms of metaphorical or analogical language to explain the significance of what Christ did and does for human beings through his incarnation, obedient life, death and resurrection, and heavenly reign, and they are to be treated seriously.

Some people suggest that penal substitution is simply one metaphor among many and that we can perhaps dispense with it or at least place it on the margin. Over against this view let me cite Trevor Hart's comment that

> the plurality of biblical imagery does not seem to be intended purely or even primarily as a selection box from which we may draw what we will according to our needs and the pre-understanding of our community . . . the metaphors are not to be understood as exchangeable, as if one might simply be substituted for another without net gain or loss, but complementary, directing us to distinct elements in and

consequences of the fullness of God's saving action in Christ and the Spirit.[16]

Likewise, Henri Blocher argues that the metaphorical language used in the New Testament does convey truth and is to be taken seriously.[17]

A second point that needs to be made is that the various metaphors used in the New Testament intermingle with one another and cannot be rigorously separated from one another. It follows that no single one of them can bear the whole weight of explaining the significance of the work of Christ. Consequently, those who criticize the metaphor of penal substitution because it cannot express every aspect of the doctrine have misunderstood the complex nature of Biblical metaphor. We should not ask this explanation of one major aspect of the death of Christ to do things that it was never intended to do.

The language of judgement, wrath and punishment

My quotation from Alan Mann, cited earlier, stated that the cross is concerned "with the restoration of a mutual, undistorted, unpolluted divine/human relationship, and not with the appeasing of a God angered by the misdeeds of his creatures." The question is: Why does this divine/human relationship need to be restored if it is not because God is angered by the misdeeds of his creatures? How else are relationships broken? Why was the death of Christ necessary

---

[16] Hart, T. "Redemption and fall." In *The Cambridge Companion to Christian Doctrine*, edited by C. E. Gunton. Cambridge: CUP, 1997, 189–206 (190). Hart himself appears to favor the "satisfaction" type of understanding and thinks that the development of theories of penal substitution was not free from some misunderstanding of Scripture (201–202).

[17] Blocher, H. "Biblical metaphors and the doctrine of the atonement," *JETS* 47:4 (Dec. 2004): 629–645. See also Blocher, H. "*Agnus Victor*: The Atonement as Victory and Vicarious Punishment." In *What Does It Mean To Be Saved? Broadening Evangelical Horizons on Salvation*, edited by J. G. Stackhouse, Jr. Grand Rapids, MI: Baker, 2002, 67–91. Also "The Sacrifice of Jesus Christ: The Current Theological Situation." *EJT* 8:1 (1999): 23–36.

to restore the relationship? I want to clarify the language of anger and appeasement but to do so in a way that will enable us all to say: "Well, maybe terms like penalty and anger are open to misunderstanding, but properly understood they express the heart of the matter."[18]

This is true in terms of the sheer volume of evidence pointing in this direction. The reality of final judgement as the active response of God to human sin is an absolutely central part of the predicament from which sinners need to be saved. No amount of emphasis on the present effects of sin and the need for salvation from them can alter the facts that, in the last analysis, "the wages of sin is death" and that we need both aspects of the "double cure": deliverance from the effects of sin as well as deliverance from the power of sin. There is a complex network of terminology that conveys this picture of judgement and condemnation.

Punishment

Admittedly the vocabulary of punishment does not figure all that prominently in the New Testament and those who would downplay the term "penal" understood in terms of punishment can point to this fact.[19] A half-dozen is the sum total of references to divine punishment, and they are associated particularly with the day of judgement:[20] In the parabolic teaching of Jesus, wicked servants will be punished when the master returns (Matt. 24:43–51; Luke 12:45–48). The

---

[18] Probably the term "appeasement" is too compromised to be usable, since it is very hard to use it of a God who takes the initiative in offering salvation to sinful human beings.

[19] In English versions sometimes words more expressive of judgement are translated by terms for punishment since the judgement implies condemnation and subsequent sentence.

[20] The term is used in some translations for the extended rebuke effected probably by some kind of excommunication of an offender at Corinth which should by now have led to his repentance (2 Cor. 2:6). If Peter regards the secular authorities as appointed by God, then they are his agents in carrying out punishment on wrongdoers (1 Pet. 2:14). Fear produces punishment (the painful feelings of anticipation of punishment to come; 1 John 4:18). Note also Hebrews 12:5–6 of the painful punishment involved in the training of children.

noun is applied once in the Gospels to the eternal punishment of the wicked (Matt. 25:46). Paul describes once how those who disobey and reject the gospel will pay the penalty of eternal destruction (2 Thess. 1:9). A person who rejects the Son of God and the blood of the covenant deserves a greater punishment than somebody who rejected the law of Moses and was put to death (Heb. 10:29). The Lord keeps the unrighteous for punishment at the day of judgement (2 Pet. 2:9).[21]

One might well be tempted at this stage to ask whether the comparative rareness of this term should warn us against putting the term "penal" in a central position in our doctrine. But to do so would be premature.

Vengeance

Second, there is the concept of vengeance, sometimes rendered as "revenge." In the Old Testament, there is the ghastly story of Adoni-Bezek who, when he is maimed by the Israelites by the amputation of his thumbs and big toes, comments: "Seventy kings with their thumbs and big toes cut off have picked up scraps under my table. Now God has paid me back for what I did to them" (Judg. 1:7). The author of Judges himself refers to God repaying the wickedness done on another occasion by Abimelek by letting him be slain by his armor-bearer (Judg. 9:56).

In the New Testament, the terminology (*ekdikēsis, ekdikeō*) can be used without this sense of repaying a person in kind for the evil that they have done. Sometimes people who are suffering injustice simply want to have their rights recognized over against an adversary by stopping the injustice and effecting some kind of compensation. So the unjust judge in the parable is a picture of those who afflict the chosen people of God, and he will intervene on their side (Luke 18:1–8). Here the emphasis would seem to be on the righting of their wrongs.

---

[21] Or "while waiting for the day of judgement" (cf. NRSV).

But vengeance may also include the common desire to inflict some corresponding pain on the wrongdoer.[22] Interestingly, and significantly, persons who want to take vengeance for evils they have suffered are commanded not to do so as private individuals but to leave it to God who will repay their opponents (Rom. 12:19; citing Deut. 32:35).[23] They are specifically not to repay the evil they have suffered by inflicting evil themselves. Human vengeance is liable to be sinful and, therefore, is prohibited, just as very firm limits are also set to the display of human anger.

In 1 Thessalonians 4:6, Paul says that God will take vengeance on those who wrong their brothers, by taking the side of the wronged and acting against the wrong-doer. Sometimes he may do this through human agents.[24] Luke 21:22 speaks about days of vengeance on Jerusalem, apparently as punishment for the people's rejection of God. In 2 Thessalonians 1:8, Paul says that God inflicts vengeance on those who do not know him and who disobey the gospel (cf. Rev. 19:2).[25]

---

[22] The principle is clear in Acts 7:24, where Stephen recounts that when an Israelite was being mistreated by an Egyptian, Moses came, overcame the attacker and did vengeance for the victim by striking (fatally) the Egyptian. We see here the element of intervention on behalf of a victim which goes beyond stopping the attack to taking the wrongdoer's life in view of his attempted murder. The principle that whoever sheds a person's blood, his blood shall be shed is here at work. But this principle may be transformed into the principle that only by carrying out such a penalty on the murderer can the community sufficiently express its disapproval of what has been done.

[23] The same Old Testament background is summoned in Hebrews 10:30 to warn that God will judge those among his people who reject his Son.

[24] In Romans 13:4, the magistrate is God's agent to carry out vengeance/ punishment, translated in the NET Bible as "'retribution,'" on wrongdoers. Similarly, Paul expresses readiness to "punish" (lit. avenge) every act of disobedience in the church at Corinth (2 Cor. 10:6); this sounds like punishment of the disobedience by one who has authority on behalf of God.

[25] In Revelation 6:10, the souls of martyrs ask God to judge and so avenge their blood. Here something is to be done make up for their murder, presumably punishment of the wrong-doers. The prayer is answered according to the expression of praise in Revelation 19:2 which describes what God has done.

Vengeance is often understood simply in terms of gaining revenge, which is the fulfillment of the personal desire that the person who makes me suffer should suffer in a corresponding manner. This crude practice should be replaced by a communal disapproval of the action of causing suffering, a disapproval that is expressed in the application of an appropriate penalty.

Wrath

The impression of sparsity that we gain from looking at punishment and vengeance is dispelled when we take note of the very much more frequent usage of the concepts of wrath and judgement. Two word groups are involved.[26]

Two Greek nouns are used for "wrath" and "anger." The first word group consists of the noun *orgē* "wrath, anger" and related words.[27] John the Baptist spoke of a future wrath (Matt. 3:7 par. Luke 3:7); Jesus could feel anger at the hardness of the human heart (Mark 3:5; cf. the use of the verb in Mark 1:41 TNIV txt.); God's wrath remains on those who reject the Son (John 3:36). There is also a lengthy set of references in the Pauline Epistles to God's future (but to some extent already revealed and active) wrath, and it is from this future wrath that believers will be saved (Rom. 5:9).[28] It is anticipated in the reaction of magistrates (as agents of God) to wrong-doing (Rom. 13:4–5). It hangs over evil-doers (Eph. 2:3; 5:6; Col. 3:6), and it comes upon unbelieving Israel for hindering evangelism of Gentiles (1 Thess. 2:16).[29] Hebrews 3:11; 4:3 cites Psalm 95:11 when talking about God's attitude

---

[26] All that needed to be said was said by Morris, L. *The Apostolic Preaching of the Cross.* London: Tyndale Press, 1965³, 179–184. Cf. Tasker, R. V. G. *The Biblical Doctrine of the Wrath of God.* London: Tyndale Press, 1951.

[27] This paucity in use of the verb may be significant in avoiding the danger of thinking of God as exercising angry passions like human beings.

[28] Cf. 1 Thessalonians 1:10; 5:9; Romans 2:5, 8; 3:5 [it is just]; 4:15 (effect of God's law); 9:22 (seen in action against "the vessels of wrath").

[29] Human anger is more or less totally forbidden (Rom. 12:19); action against enemies should be left to God (cf. Eph. 4:31; Col. 3:8; 1 Tim. 2:8; Titus 1:7; Jas. 1:19–20).

to disobedient Israel, and this citation provides me with a peg on which I can hang the reminder that references to God's anger in the Old Testament can be counted in their hundreds. Revelation particularly emphasizes the coming expression of the wrath of God and the Lamb (Rev. 6:16–17; 11:18; 14:10). In Revelation 14:10, the term "cup" is used metaphorically for suffering and especially for suffering imposed by God as a result of his wrath (cf. Mark 10:39–39; 14:36).[30]

The other term for wrath, *thumos*,[31] is used by Paul for a human passion that is to be avoided (2 Cor. 12:20; Gal. 5:20; Eph. 4:31; Col. 3:8), and by Revelation for the wrath of the devil (Rev. 12:12) and the passion of the harlot (Rev. 14:8). It is also used in Revelation for various expressions of the powerful wrath of God against the evil world (Rev. 14:10, 19; 15:1, 7; 16:1, 19; 19:15).

Judgement

Far more common than these concepts of punishment and wrath is the use of the concept of judgement. It is no exaggeration to say that it is part of the framework of thought in the majority of New Testament books.[32] It is simply taken for granted. And it becomes thematic particularly in Matthew; John; Romans; Hebrews; James; 1 Peter; 2 Peter; Jude; Revelation.

In the Synoptic Gospels it is said that God has appointed his Son to be Judge, and that we shall all appear before his judgement seat to be judged justly for what we have done. This occasion is referred to as a "day of judgement" (Matt. 10:15; 11:22, 24; 12:36)[33] or simply "the judgement" (Matt.

---

[30] For the view that the cup is associated with God's wrath, see especially Cranfield, C. E. B. *The Gospel according to Saint Mark.* Cambridge: CUP, 1977[5], 337–339.

[31] The verb is used only once, with reference to King Herod (Matt. 2:16).

[32] The vocabulary is absent from Mark; Galatians; Ephesians; Philippians; Colossians; 1 Thessalonians; Titus; Philemon; 2 John; 3 John, but, with the exception of the tiny books, other expressions are used to convey the same essential reality.

[33] The conjunction of "day" and "judgement" is probably due to Matthaean redaction; cf. Luke 10:12 which simply has "the day."

5:21–22; 12:41–42 par. Luke 11:31–32), which may involve condemnation to Gehenna (Matt. 23:33). Other references to judgement are found in Matthew 7:1 par. Luke 6:37; Luke 19:22 (parabolic).[34]

Future judgement through Christ is mentioned once in Acts 17:31. Although Jesus was not sent into the world to judge it (John 3:17–18; 12:47–48), nevertheless, there is a sense in which judgement is already taking place (John 3:18b; 8:16; 16:11), and future judgement at the resurrection of the dead has been committed to him (John 5:22–30). The Pauline writings have the same horizon of a future judgement by God (Rom 14:10–12) on a specific "day" (Rom. 2:16), carried out by Christ (2 Cor. 5:10; 2 Thess. 1:7–8; 2 Tim. 4:1). It embraces the world (Rom. 3:6), both Jews (Rom. 2:12) and Gentiles (cf. 1 Cor. 5:13), believers and unbelievers (Rom. 14:10). There is a present activity which appears to have more the function of warning people against behavior which, if persisted in, will lead to a worse fate in the future (1 Cor. 11:32).[35] It will condemn those who have refused to believe the truth (2 Thess. 2:12).

Similar teaching is found elsewhere in the New Testament. Hebrews also has the horizon of future judgement by God (Heb. 9:27; 10:27, 30; 13:4), as do James (Jas. 2:12–13; 5:9), 1 Peter (1 Pet. 1:17; 4:5–6), 2 Peter (2 Pet. 2:9; 3:7), Jude (Jude 15), and Revelation (Rev. 6:10; 11:18; 14:7; 18:8, 20; 19:2, 11; 20:12–13).

Destruction and death

Finally, in this list of expressions concerning judgement and punishment, the outcome of various sins is expressed in terms of destruction and death.

---

[34] The Twelve will judge the twelve tribes of Israel (Matt. 19:28 par. Luke. 22:30), but this may refer to rule rather than to a judicial function.

[35] Although there is a future judgement of believers, it is a moot point whether eternal condemnation is an option for them, most arguing that it is concerned with reward and loss rather than justification and rejection.

Like judgement, this concept of destruction is extraordinarily pervasive in the New Testament. The broad road leads to destruction (Matt. 7:13); God destroys body and soul in Gehenna (Matt. 10:28 par. Luke 12:4); the ultimate end of those who reject the kingdom of God or do not repent is the destruction of their life or soul, with destruction and salvation being juxtaposed as opposite fates (Mark 8:35 par. Matt. 10:39 par. Luke 9:24-25; Matt. 16:25 par. Luke 17:33 par. John 12:25; cf. Luke 13:3, 5; John 3:16); sinners (Rom. 2:12), the so-called "vessels of wrath" (Rom. 9:22), are intended for destruction; the opponents of the gospel and enemies of the cross share the same fate (Phil. 1:28; 3:19; cf. 2 Pet. 2:1, 3; 3:7, 16); those who are not saved are described as "those who are being destroyed," i.e., who are on their way to final destruction (1 Cor. 1:18; 2 Cor. 2:15; 4:3; 2 Thess. 2:10; cf. Jas. 4:12; 2 Pet. 3:9; Jude 5).

And there is the concept of death, both physical and ultimate. The outcome of various sins is being sent to Gehenna by God himself (Matt. 10:28; Luke 12:5). The concept of torment is found occasionally, both in the imagery of some of the parables (Matt. 18:34; Luke 16:23, 28) and also in the description of the lake of fire in Revelation where it is the destination for the devil and his agents (Rev. 14:10-11; 18:7; 20:10). I believe that it would be wrong to take the imagery to imply that God behaves in a way that would arouse the criticism of a cosmic equivalent of Amnesty International or similar agencies.

The New Testament concept of future judgement

So far I have simply been listing references without much interpretation. But this compilation of the evidence leads to three significant conclusions:

1. The framework of thought in the New Testament clearly presupposes the future judgement of God against evil-doers, expressed in the display of his wrath against sin and the destruction or death of sinners.

2. There is no other kind of future scenario or description of the attitude and actions of God. This is not one type of metaphorical description among others. And there is no indication of a universalism in which all are saved and none are ultimately condemned.[36]
3. This teaching is more than just a background of thought. It becomes thematic on many occasions, and it lies at the centre of the evangelism carried out in the early church, where salvation was understood as including deliverance from the wrath of God and eternal death.[37] Consequently, we cannot push it to one side as being less important than the other aspects of human sin and need.

But now we reach the really contentious issue. There have been numerous attempts to argue that this wrath is not the divine equivalent of what, in human terms, would be a feeling or emotion, still less an arbitrary outburst of rage. Some would understand it simply in terms of the inevitable self-inflicted wounds of sin that God allows to happen. However, I can see no legitimate way of avoiding the fact that these terms refer to the attitude of God himself that results in action being taken against sinners. The following points are decisive:

1. To some extent, but certainly not entirely, God's wrathful actions may be the ways in which the results of sinning affect the sinners themselves; they can be said to bring calamity upon themselves. But I would deny the conclusion that to speak in this way is to say that the calamity is not brought about by God. So, when Stephen Travis describes the nature of the wrath in Romans 1 as "God's allowing of people to experience the intrinsic consequences of their refusal to live in relationship with him," and contrasts this with "the retributive inflicting of punishment from

---

[36] See various of the essays (including my own) in *Universal Salvation? The Current Debate,* edited by R. Parry and C. Partridge. Carlisle: Paternoster Press, 2003.

[37] The distribution of the various words and word-groups can be seen from the following table.

	Mt	Mk	Lk	Jn	Ac	Ro	1C	2C	Ga	Ep	Ph	Co	1Th	2Th	PE	He	Js	1P	2P	1J	Jd	Rv
Punish	*		*					*						*		*			*	*		
Wrath	*		*	*		*				*		*	*			*						*
Judge	*	*	*	*	*	*	*	*		*		*		*	*			*	*	*	*	*
Cup	*	*	*																			
Gehenna	*	*	*														*					
Destroy	*	*	*	*	*	*	*	*	*		*		*	*	*	*	*		*		*	*
Death						*	*	*					*	*		*	*			*		*
Curse									*													

PE – Pastoral Epistles

outside,"[38] this is a false antithesis in that it ignores the precise "*God* gave them up" language of Paul.

2. The parallel language of judgement describes God, whether the Father or the Son, as the person who brings about this fate of sinners. The imagery employed is that of a specific day or time when God carries out his judgement; this strongly implies a deliberate action of God, rather than a continuous, impersonal process. In this context, the language of wrath is perfectly at home. It is appropriate for a judge to express the wrath felt by society against unrepentant, convicted criminals by saying how people feel about their callous and cruel behavior. If God is the personal agent in judgement, then, equally, he is the personal agent of wrath, particularly since it is so frequently referred to as *his* wrath.

3. The personal reaction of God is also present in the context of reconciliation. Here the language of broken personal relationships (enmity) is appropriate. The fact that, after rebellious sinners accept what Christ has done for them, God no longer reckons their sins against them indicates that before that point he did so reckon them and, therefore, he would treat them as rebels and liable to whatever should befall them. If his attitude and behavior after the acceptance of reconciliation is personal, so too is his attitude before it. And indeed it is because it is personal that it issues in his offer of reconciliation.

4. If God is said in Scripture to feel other emotions, such as tender compassion, it is difficult to see how he cannot feel some kind of revulsion against evil. If God can be said to bring his wrath to an end or to turn from it (Exod. 32:12; 2 Chr. 12:12; Ps. 37:8; Hab. 3:2), then equally he can begin it (cf. Rom. 3:5; 9:22) or refuse to exercise it (1 Thess. 5:9) It is something that is under his control.

To deny that God feels some kind of negative feeling about sin is a denial of the personal character of God who reacts to the evil that ruins his creation and destroys his relationship with his creatures. It is to make the divine

---

[38] Travis, "Christ as Bearer of Divine Judgment," 338.

judgement something impersonal and mechanistic rather than the personal reaction of the living God. If we allow that God feels pain when he sees his creatures suffer, equally we must allow that he feels disappointment extending to wrath against those who cause the suffering. So, for example, when Green and Baker say that human acts of wickedness "do not arouse the wrath of God but are themselves already the consequences of its active presence,"[39] they fail to see that it was precisely God's wrath that led to these consequences of sin.

5. God's wrath is not arbitrary, uncontrolled rage. There is a tendency on the part of critics to understanding the divine feeling of wrath by analogy with a human emotion. Human anger may be arbitrary: it may burst out for no reasonable cause, it may be uncontrolled and intemperate and not know when to stop, it may be disproportionate to the offence, and it may be irrational in that it somehow gives satisfaction to the wrathful person, as when I deal with my frustration by shouting at my computer. Whatever we may make of some of the more difficult material in the Old Testament, which I leave to others more competent than myself to discuss, the New Testament does not ascribe such arbitrariness and selfish, uncontrolled anger to God. To use such a term as "fury," although it is found in Scripture, is to run the risk of misunderstanding. When Paul forbids the human activity of taking vengeance and says "leave it to God," it does not follow that divine vengeance is exercised in the same sorts of ways as sinful, human vengeance would be.

---

[39] Green and Baker, *Recovering*, 55, make a contrast between God striking out in vengeance against sinners and letting people suffer the consequences which are inherent in their own sins. But this does not take into account passages that speak of God's action subsequent to human sin (2 Thess. 1:6-9) or God expressing his wrath (Rom. 3:5), or God wishing to show his wrath (Rom. 9:22), or God's wrath coming upon disobedience (Eph. 5:6; Col. 3:6), or the Old Testament language of God swearing in his wrath that is used in Hebrews (Heb. 3:11; 4:3), or God carrying out judgement. The term "vengeance" is not the best one for the holy response of God to sin, but the notion that God does not act in reaction to sin is false.

6. It is sometimes said that wrath is not fundamental to the character of God in the way that love is. It is true that wrath is kindled as a reaction to evildoers, but it is equally the case that mercy is kindled as a reaction to pitiable people. The criticism arises from failing to observe that love and wrath are not on the same level. The fundamental character of God is expressed in terms of love and holiness (or righteousness). Both qualities express themselves in secondary ways in response to human sin, namely grace (or mercy) and wrath. You may say, if you will, that the wrath is called forth only when evil is present and to that extent is not fundamental, but precisely the same thing could be said about God's grace which is necessitated only when sin causes his creatures to need it.

But, granted that Romans 1 shows that one form of judgement is the direct outworking of the sin itself, it must be insisted that this is not the only form and, in this case, a line between what God allows or permits and what he directly sanctions seems to me to be non-existent.[40] God is as responsible for what he allows (assuming that he has power to cause things to happen otherwise) as for what he directly wills.

Accordingly, the metaphor being used is that of wrath as the human response to persons who do things of which we disapprove. It is the attitude of strong disapproval that may be expressed in a withdrawal of affection and an attitude of displeasure that is intended to make the culprits feel uncomfortable and wish that they had not done the wrong action. But again, it must be emphasized that, when the language is used of God, we must carefully remove from this complex human attitude those elements which are themselves sinful, such as the overreaction in a fit of temper that gets out of control; the use of words like revenge and even vengeance; the use of superior power to crush the offender. A sinless expression of wrath, free from the elements that

---

[40] Later, I shall suggest that there is a sense in which the response of God is the direct outworking of the sin.

disfigure human wrath, is perfectly conceivable and proper to use of God.

Hence, to say that "wrath is not a divine property or essential attribute of God,"[41] is, to my mind, a basic error that leads to a mistaken understanding of the cross. The God of the Bible and the God of the New Testament is fundamentally holy and loving, and both of these attributes are relational; they find expression in grace and mercy towards his creation and yet also judgement and wrath when that creation is spoilt by sin.

The nature of judgement and penalties

How are wrath and judgement actually expressed against the offender? In the human sphere, justice is the upholding of right against evil not simply by asserting the principle, but by taking action against the offender, the latter action being termed "judgement." The terms "punishment," "penalty," and "sentence" are commonly used to refer to this action or experience. These terms may cover a number of elements, not all of which are necessarily present on each occasion.[42] This now raises the question of the nature of the judgemental reaction of wrath. Strong voices have been raised in recent years in favor of a fresh understanding of the purpose of human penalties and punishment. There is something of a dialectic here. A major concern is the revaluation of the purposes and aims of human criminal justice, and it could be argued that this provides an analogy in the light of which we can understand divine justice. Alternatively, it might be argued, for example, that divine justice is the model upon which human justice is to be shaped. Either way, arguments can be offered for the inherently retributive nature of the penalties for offences.

Human punishment can, and normally does, include a complex of various elements.

---

[41] Green and Baker, *Recovering*, 54.
[42] See the discussion by Marshall, C. D. *Beyond Retribution* for details.

Restraint and deterrence

These terms refer to actions taken to prevent evil deeds recurring. The actions taken are either some kind of restriction on the original offender to prevent a repetition of the crime or a warning to potential offenders. Detention in prison, or some other form of restraint, may be necessary to stop the offender re-offending. Or, there may be some form of penalty imposed upon the offender that will also act as a warning to others who may be tempted to similar crimes. A penalty, such as a fine, will induce offenders not to offend in future. Unfortunately, a notice that says "trespassers will be forgiven" will be much less effective.

Reformation

At a deeper level, the penalty imposed may be designed to educate and reform offenders so that, quite apart from fear of the consequences, they will see the wrongness and folly of their actions, and resolve to live differently. Ideally, we should like to see wrongdoers *repent* of the wrong that they have done and resolve to live lives free of wrongdoing from this point on. In practice, however, we have to be realistic and recognize that this happens less frequently than we would wish, and perhaps the majority of people, including ourselves, keep the laws because we are afraid of being caught and penalized if we do not keep them. Consequently, human systems have to operate on the assumption that they will seldom completely achieve their intended ends.

In both of these ways, the aim of having a just society free from crime is being pursued by practical means.[43]

Guilt

This raises the further question whether there is more to justice than these two aspects, neither of which is strictly

---

[43] Restraint, deterrence, and reformation are closely related, all being intended to prevent the criminal or potential criminals from committing further crimes. Some would argue that these aspects are not strictly-speaking punitive. They are, however, part of the way in which the community or law-giver endeavors to uphold the rule of law and prevent law-breaking.

concerned with *justice* as a principle. It is in this context that the concept of *guilt* arises. It is a concept with three associated meanings.

1. "Guilty" is a term used to refer to or identify a person who has actually committed a particular offence, rather than somebody who has not done so. When a court establishes that a person is guilty, that simply means "it has been sufficiently established that he/she did it," and when a person is acquitted, that simply means "he/she did not do it," or perhaps "it cannot be sufficiently established that he/she did it."
2. "Guilt" may refer to the feeling of the person who has committed an offence. It involves feelings of being blameworthy ("I should have driven more carefully"), and moral failure ("I am ashamed of what I have done").
3. There is the understanding of "guilt" as a state from which a person can be delivered only by some act of restitution and/or retribution which is understood to cancel out the offence so that it is no longer counted against the person. This is the sense that concerns us here.

Restitution and retribution

The crucial question concerns what (if anything) the guilty offender may have to do in order for the offence to be no longer counted against him or her. It is commonly held that something should be required from the offender to compensate for the crime. This can take two forms.

The first (*restitution*) is when the offender is required to do something that undoes (so far as possible) the effects of the crime (for example, restoring stolen property; paying for medical treatment for the victim of assault). If this is not possible, the offender is required to give some kind of compensation (like paying money to a maimed person), or otherwise doing some good to society as a whole (community service). Any of these options will be at some personal cost in time, effort, and money. The underlying principles emerging here are that justice requires that the crime be undone so far as is possible, and that, if possible, this should be done by the guilty person (although it might also be done by the community). Simply punishing the offender does not undo the effects of the crime for the victim.

In passing, it should be noted that, in some societies, the *honor* of a person is thought to be affected and diminished by a crime, and it is held that the offender should make some kind of satisfaction to restore that honor. Some such idea lies behind the Anselmian type of understanding of the death of Christ. Perhaps it underlies the principle that if a person kills another human being, then by a human being shall that person's blood be shed (Gen. 9:6). The concept lingers on in the attitude we take to so-called "contempt of court," but, on the whole, the weaknesses of this approach are now well appreciated.

The second type of requirement (*retribution*) arises when it is laid down that if a person causes somebody else to suffer, then they should be made to *suffer proportionately* to cancel out the original evil deed. The offender may pay an arbitrarily fixed fine[44] or serve time in prison. Here the thought is not just that the person must suffer something to bring home to them the fact of their crime as crime, but also that, in some sense, the crime has not been "paid for" until the criminal has suffered something comparable to the suffering that they have caused. This is most clearly so in the case of murder where murderers are either subjected to loss of their own life or deprived of liberty for a so-called life sentence; the thought is that a life must be paid for with a life.[45] Until the penalty has been paid, the guilty person remains guilty.

Where the penalty coincides with making restitution for the crime to the victim, or to society more generally, there is nothing problematic here. But, in many cases, where restitution is not possible (or the practice has not been developed), there may simply be the infliction of pain and loss upon the criminal, and the penalty is purely retributory.

---

[44] It is virtually impossible to assign a monetary value to the pain and loss that have been suffered.

[45] Even though in practice a literal "life sentence" may not be imposed.

Difficulties arise with the latter. It does not do any good to the victim or others affected by the crime. The victim's relatives may cry out for vengeance, but it is hard to see how making the offender suffer actually does any good to the persons who have suffered. Nor is it clear how proportionate suffering by the offender undoes the offence. Although Adoni-Bezek saw a grim correspondence between the evil he had done and the evil done to him, it is impossible to believe that God needs to make people suffer in the same way as they have caused others to suffer, or to inflict upon them the barbarity that they have inflicted upon others, in order that he might gain some kind of self-satisfaction or upholding of an abstract principle of justice. Popular usage, however, often thinks of retribution as the imposition of proportionate suffering on the person who has caused others to suffer or simply broken the law. It is this element that seems dubious.

How, then, should retribution be understood, and why is it thought to be necessary? It is part of a total response to evil-doing which is concerned to establish and uphold a just community. This response includes:

1. The undoing of the situation caused by the offender, where somebody else is the victim
2. The development of a society in which such offences are not committed
3. The attempt to change the hearts of offenders from willfully doing what is wrong to gladly doing what is right. This is a change that will include penitence for past offences
4. The dissociation of the community from the criminal. Action is taken that shows that the community stands for justice and does not tolerate evil-doers, and, therefore, takes action to reform them. The hope is that they will repent and eschew crime; if all else fails, they will be excluded from the community. "Punishment is essentially this disowning by a community of acts done by its

members."[46] The biblical utterance "Depart from me, you workers of iniquity" sums up this attitude.

A major reason, then, for the imposition of penalties is so that *society may express its disapproval of and rejection of evil and evildoers*. It upholds justice and law, by asserting the principle that people must not disobey the laws and that doing so will have consequences. We may put lawbreakers in prison for an arbitrary period of time, a sort of temporary exclusion order, whereby we indicate to them and to the whole community that we are upholding justice (as we understand it) and will not tolerate lawbreakers in our society. There is a proper use of the principle of proportionality here.[47]

It goes almost without saying that the penalty is *painful*. It certainly is if it involves physical pain, or being deprived of something that you enjoy, such as loss of money or time. However, in some circumstances, it might be seen in a different light, as when the offender recognizes the enormity of what has been done and is happy to make restitution for the offence, even though it involves personal cost.

In the case of biblical, temporal, divine judgements, the need for restitution is clear enough in some of the Old Testament legislation, and the act of restitution can be painful. A reformatory element is present in the temporal judgements in the Old Testament; it is successful when the people of Israel collectively recognize that their sin has landed them in trouble and they turn back to God. It must be remembered here that the thought is not simply of the reformation of individuals but of the nation as a whole; even

---

[46] Hodgson, L. *The Doctrine of the Atonement*. London: Nisbet, 1951, 57. The Old Testament also knows the idea that the land itself is polluted by the crimes that take place in it, and hence the sacrificial system is concerned with the removal of that pollution as well as the restoration of the sinful person.

[47] Certainly, if we took James 2:10 seriously, we would argue that any person who commits adultery is actually guilty of the much more serious and basic sin of disobedience to the law as divine command, and, therefore, any individual sin is equally culpable, but on the human level we recognize that this is unjust and proportionality is unavoidable.

though some people die as a result of judgement, the effect may be reformatory on the survivors and "the nation" is put right with God.

However, in the case of the final judgement, as it is traditionally understood (never-ending punishment or eternal death), reformation of the sinner is, by definition, excluded. The elements of deterrence (by the prospect and warning) and restraint (in that the sinner is no longer able to commit acts of sin) are present. At first sight, the element of restitution may seem to be absent. The need for it may be seen in the way in which, after the holocaust, genocide, and other contemporary forms of violent and murderous behavior, it has been recognized that it is not enough to deal with the offenders, but that there must also be some kind of healing for the families of the victims. Similarly, there is an element of healing in the salvation that is offered by God in Christ; he wipes away the tears of all who mourn and comforts them (Rev. 21:4; Matt. 5:5).

The punitive element here is described not only as eternal destruction,[48] but also as separation from the presence of the Lord (2 Thess. 1:9). These two elements are different aspects of expressing the same action, and it is the latter which expresses the rationale of the action and is the decisive one. The main element accordingly is the exclusion of sinners from the holy society and the presence of the holy God. This is what is signified by the term "retribution," although the latter is often popularly understood more in terms of revenge or vengeance or exacting some penalty that is judged to involve suffering that is proportionate to the sin.[49]

---

[48] I would be more inclined to argue that this does not mean eternal, conscious punishment but rather final, irreversible destruction than I was when I listed these possibilities in an earlier publication. See Marshall, I. H. *1 and 2 Thessalonians*. London: Marshall, Morgan and Scott, 1983, 178–180.

[49] Moule, C. F. D. "Punishment and Retribution" in his *Essays in New Testament Interpretation*. Cambridge: CUP, 1982, 235–49; without denying that "dire consequences are attached to sin" (242), he questions the need to retain the motif of retribution (and with it of penal substitution) in Christian theology. He recognizes the existence of passages expressing

I would therefore defend the proposition that, in the divine-human context, the ultimate element in judgement is the *exclusion from the community*, from the kingdom of God, of those who rebel against God and disobey his commandments.[50] The Son of Man says, "Depart from me" (Matt. 25:41); this statement combines the two essential elements of upholding righteousness and of excluding those who do not do so. Retribution means, of course, that this penalty is carried out on those who have done wrong and not on the innocent. The biblical principles are that whatever we sow we shall also reap (Gal. 6:7), and that we receive the due "reward" or "wage" of our sins (Rom. 1:27; 6:23; 2 Cor. 5:10; 11:15; 2 Pet. 2:12–13; Rev. 18:6). This is painful, and it is brought about ultimately by God.[51] In other words, something happens to sinners as a result of the sins for which they are responsible. It is an appropriate result because the sinners have rejected God and his rule, and there can be no place for such in his just and compassionate community.

But is this rightly termed "retribution"? Retribution refers to the reaction against the specific offender without specifying what is involved in the reaction.[52] Strictly speaking, this term conveys the idea that if somebody commits an offence, then the reaction of the judge[53] is directed against the offender in respect of their offence/attitude; it implies the necessity

---

retribution in the New Testament but argues that they are "peripheral and alien to a strict exposition of the Gospel" (242).

[50] Cf. Williams, G. "The Cross and the Punishment of Sin." In *Where Wrath and Mercy Meet*, edited by Peterson, 90–94. The concept of exclusion has a parallel in the Old Testament concept of exile as exclusion from the promised land of those who have broken the covenant, and some theologians want to understand "Christ's death on the cross as the divine punishment of exile" (Boersma, H. *Violence, Hospitality and the Cross; Reappropriating the Atonement Tradition*. Grand Rapids, MI: Baker, 2004, 19, 174–177).

[51] Cf. Blocher. "Sacrifice," 32.

[52] A dictionary definition (COD) is: "recompense usually for evil done, vengeance, requital". Earlier theological discussion is summarized in Towner, W. S. "Retribution." *IDB Sup.*: 742–44.

[53] This term is used on occasion for God or Christ and is supplemented by a much larger number of references to God or Christ fulfilling this function.

of proceeding against each offender and not against other people not involved in the offence. Retribution should be understood to mean the action taken against offenders in order to uphold justice, to restrain evildoers, to undo so far as may be possible the effects of the offence, and, where the evildoer is irreformable, to exclude that person from the community and its benefits.[54] Since, in this specific case, the exclusion is exclusion from the blessings of the kingdom of God, it follows that this exclusion is experienced as painful by those who undergo it. I do not see how deprivation of eternal life can be understood as anything other than a penalty or punishment upon the impenitent sinner.[55]

Behind our simple talk about the "penalty" of sin are two things. On the one hand, we can speak about the painful consequences of sin, both for the sinners and for their victims. This thought is wider than that of the legal penalty and brings into consideration the whole set of miserable consequences of sin to which God gives sinners up, in the hope that this may lead to repentance. On the other hand, there is the divine upholding of justice and love and the exclusion of those who persist in injustice and lack of love. The ultimate form of such exclusion is depicted in the imagery of hell, death, and destruction.

Although the terms "penal" and "penalty" are rare in the New Testament, they can be understood to refer to the whole breadth of the consequences of sin,[56] rather than simply in legal terms. We can thus attain a more biblical understanding of the concept of retribution. This stands against the popular notion often seeming to consist in making a person suffer

---

[54] My impression is that theologians use this term without defining and analyzing it to any extent. Packer's article uses it but does not discuss it.

[55] On the impossibility of avoiding "violence" in this fallen universe, see especially Boersma, *Violence*.

[56] The flight from the language of penalty is by no means universal. Among theologians who continue to speak of wrath and punishment I note Hooker, M. D. *Not Ashamed of the Gospel: New Testament Interpretations of the Death of Christ*. Carlisle: Paternoster Press, 1994, 43; earlier Hodgson, L. *The Doctrine of the Atonement*. London: Nisbet, 1951, 52–67; Künneth, W. *The Theology of the Resurrection*. London: SCM Press, 1965, 155.

until, in some arbitrary way, they have suffered what we regard as appropriate for their offence. In this way we may be able to progress to a better understanding of what human justice ought to achieve, and equally a better understanding of the nature of divine justice. Judgement on wrongdoing and wrongdoers is concerned with the upholding of righteousness by the community or its ruler(s), the exclusion in one way or another of those who reject its moral standards, making restitution for the effects of sin where this is possible, and the restoration of penitent and repentant wrongdoers.

We can now see, incidentally, that the divine response to sin is a condign penalty in that at the heart of sin lies a rejection of God and his will for his creation, expressed in his commandments of love for him and for one another. To disobey God and rebel against him is to break the personal relationship with God, and thus in a sense to cut oneself off from him. Thus it is appropriate for God to respond to those who cut themselves off from him by excluding them from his kingdom. Final judgement is the execution of such a penalty after God, in his mercy, has provided a way of salvation that has been persistently refused and rejected.

2 The Substitutionary Death of Jesus

The holiness and love of God: the nature of atonement

Why does the New Testament speak of God excluding sinners from his presence and from his kingdom? It is because it lies in the character of God that he is holy (or righteous) and loving. Ultimately, the holiness and the love are inseparable facets of the same character, but, since we have no English term that expresses both these qualities simultaneously, it is necessary to use both words in order to make it clear that God's character cannot be reduced simply to one quality or the other. The concept of human fatherhood in the ancient world included and required both of these ideas; the father is the upholder of justice within the family (1 Pet. 1:17) and simultaneously the compassionate and loving carer for the family. It is not strange, then, that they are both aspects of divine fatherhood. God's love wants to see justice done, and his justice requires that people be loved.

With the recognition of God's fundamental character in this way, we begin to move from a consideration of God's judgement upon sinners to his action to undo the effects of their sin and to mend the breach that this has caused.

The classical theologian who has done most to present a carefully wrought doctrine of atonement that takes holiness fully into account is P. T. Forsyth. He has been called evangelicalism's greatest modern theologian of the cross,[1]

---

[1] David Bebbington, cited by L. McCurdy in his article in *The Dictionary of Historical Theology*, edited by T. A. Hart. Carlisle: Paternoster Press/ Grand Rapids, MI: Eerdmans, 2000, 217–218. See McCurdy's full treatment,

although that title must surely be shared with his fellow Scot, the New Testament scholar, James Denney. Forsyth seems to be overlooked by some of the critics of penal substitution[2] as well as by its defenders,[3] but he is a central player in this discussion. With the following summary of his position we shall begin to move at last from a discussion of the nature of the penalty to an understanding of the divine response.

Forsyth laid what may seem to be extraordinary emphasis on the holiness as well as the love of God, so much so that he wrote frequently about holy love. And he left us in no doubt that the holiness of God must figure centrally in any doctrine of the atonement: "By the atonement, therefore, is meant that action of Christ's death which has a prime regard to God's holiness, has it for its first charge, and finds man's reconciliation impossible except as that holiness is divinely satisfied once for all on the cross. Such an atonement is the key to the incarnation."[4]

It follows that the notion of judgement is inescapable: "The idea of God's holiness is inseparable from the idea of judgement as the mode by which grace goes into action."[5] God had to satisfy his own holiness in dealing with the problem of human sin, and he himself did so in the holy obedience and self-offering of his Son, through which reconciliation between God and the sinful world is achieved. Alongside judgement, Forsyth upheld firmly the concept of God's wrath as the reaction of holy love to sin: "the reconciliation has no meaning apart from guilt which must stir the anger of a holy

---

Attributes and Atonement: The Holy Love of God in the Theology of P. T. Forsyth. Carlisle: Paternoster Press, 1999. Forsyth's mature thought is in his *The Work of Christ.* London: Hodder and Stoughton, 1910; London: reprinted Independent Press, 1938 and subsequently. See also *The Cruciality of the Cross.* London: Independent Press, 1909; reprinted Carlisle: Paternoster Press, 1997.

[2] But not by Smail, *Once and for all*, 45, 86–87, 98, 119, 186.

[3] But not by Leon Morris. See the index to *The Apostolic Preaching of the Cross.* London: Tyndale Press, 1965[3]. Surprisingly he is not mentioned by H. Boersma, *Violence.*

[4] *Cruciality*, viii.

[5] Cruciality, viii.

God and produce separation from Him."[6] He insisted that "we do not only grieve God but we provoke His anger,"[7] and he strenuously rejected the idea that the law was "detached from God, and cut adrift to do its own mechanic work under His indifference."[8]

"Atonement means the covering of sin by something which God Himself had provided and therefore the covering of sin by God Himself."[9] What Christ offered was "the perfect obedience of holy love which he offered amidst the conditions of sin, death and judgment." Christ made the perfect confession to God but it was "not the sympathetic confession of our sin so much as the practical confession of God's holiness."[10] "There is a penalty and curse for sin; and Christ consented to enter that region... It is impossible for us to say that God was angry with Christ; but still Christ entered the wrath of God... You can therefore say that although Christ was not punished by God, He bore God's penalty upon sin. To say that Christ was punished by God who was always well-pleased with Him is an outrageous thing. Calvin himself repudiates the idea."[11] Christ "turned the penalty He endured into sacrifice He offered. And the sacrifice He offered was the judgment He accepted."[12]

Ultimately, Forsyth sees his restatement of the doctrine as moving from an emphasis upon substitutionary expiation to what he calls "solidary reparation, consisting of due acknowledgement of God's holiness, and the honouring of that and not of His honour."[13] He suggests that "judgment is a much better word than either penalty or punishment," and interestingly he would prefer to speak of representation rather than substitution, judging that "substitution does not

---

[6] *Work*, 80.
[7] *Work*, 241.
[8] *Work*, 242.
[9] *Work*, 55.
[10] *Work*, 201.
[11] *Work*, 147.
[12] *Work*, 163.
[13] *Work*, 164–65.

take account of the moral results on the soul."[14] I take this to mean not that Forsyth rejected what is conveyed by the term substitution but that he thought that representative was the more comprehensive and appropriate term to use, conveying what is meant by substitution and more. If, however, "representative" means less than "substitute," then I have no doubt which term should be used.[15]

Here we have an exposition of the character of God which takes both holiness and wrath seriously, and that I find to be much more in tune with the teaching of the New Testament than the position of the anti-penal thinkers. The essential difference is that Forsyth, and those like him, hold on firmly to the biblical teaching about the holiness and the resulting wrath of God which issue in his active judgement of sinners. They then embrace that understanding of the Christ's work which sees it as the active obedience and expression of holiness in which God himself not only bears the painful consequences of human sin, but also his judgement upon it. So he provides the way to reconciliation with himself. To uphold holiness and righteousness, God had to be seen to be both just and the justifier, and this he did by bearing the judgement or penalty of sin himself.

L. McCurdy has argued convincingly that to talk about a conflict between God's love and his holiness is unnecessary. He claims that, while John Stott sees a conflict that God has to overcome and criticizes Forsyth's view, Forsyth himself sees what he calls a "strain." Where Stott talks about a change in God's nature, Forsyth states that God's nature did not change.[16]

Forsyth's doctrine may seem more like a theory of satisfaction than of penal substitution, and it is so categorized by T. H. Hughes in a critical evaluation that is not altogether sympathetic.[17] But since what is satisfied is God's holiness rather than his honor, Forsyth does go in a somewhat

---

[14] *Work*, 182.

[15] Cf. the discussion by Packer, "What did the cross achieve?", 22–25.

[16] McCurdy, 204–222. Cf. Stott, *Cross*.

[17] Hughes, T. H. *The Atonement: Modern Theories of the Doctrine*. London: George Allen and Unwin, 1949, 38–46.

different direction from Anselm. My understanding is that Hughes' categorization of Forsyth has not fully grasped his point, and that Forsyth gives, in fact, a classical statement of the evangelical doctrine. Indeed, I would hope that it is a statement that might help to ease the tensions that presently exist between evangelical theologians, and lead us to an understanding on which we would all substantially agree. In fact, similar things are said by theologians like Smail and Travis,[18] and I think that it is fair to say that we are close to agreement on a positive statement of the Christ's work. The crucial difference is that I see this as an exposition of what is meant by penal substitution and appeasement of God rather than as a denial of these two categories of interpretation.

The vital point that needs to be grasped is that it is impossible to separate the personal and the judicial aspects in God as the sovereign ruler. To be a judge is not necessarily to be impersonal. Somehow God has to act in such a way that his justice is upheld (Rom. 3:26). This is achieved by Christ's death which enables God to pardon sinners while upholding justice. The judgement on sinners is that God dissociates himself from them, and they are thus excluded from the family of God. There can be no greater loss than that, and it is condign for sinners who have rejected the sovereignty of God and his calling to holiness and love. I cannot see any way to regard this exclusion of sinners as anything other than the divinely-imposed consequence or penalty for sin. When the judgement upon sinners is set aside, it is done so by God on the basis of his own prevenient grace.

The underlying principle?

Forsyth's exposition has demonstrated that the penal substitution principle (or, if you will, the judgemental substitution principle) is clearly present in one way of understanding

---

[18] Smail, *Once and For All*, 93, and Travis, "Christ as Bearer of Divine Judgment in Paul's Thought about the Atonement," 344–45. Both want to argue that Christ did indeed bear the judgement upon sin but did not bear punishment.

of the death of Christ. The question is: Is it principal and determinative throughout the New Testament? Let us consider the various metaphors of atonement:

Sacrifice

Sacrificial language is widespread in the New Testament.[19] It is present in the Gospel of John with its understanding of the Lamb of God bearing the sins of the world (John 1:29, cf. 1 John 3:5).[20] 1 John uses the language of atoning sacrifice

---

[19] Various scholars have attempted to play down its significance for Paul. Cf. Hahn, F. *Der urchristliche Gottesdienst.* Stuttgart: Verlag Katholische Bibelwerk, 1970, 53 n. 29; McLean, B. H. *The Cursed Christ: Mediterranean Expulsion Ritual and Pauline Soteriology.* Sheffield: Sheffield Academic Press, 1996; McLean, B. H. "The absence of an atoning sacrifice in Paul's soteriology." *NTS* 38 (1992): 531–55. On the place of sacrifice in the Bible generally, see Beckwith R. T., and M. J. Selman (eds.), *Sacrifice in the Bible.* Carlisle: Paternoster Press, 1995.

[20] To "bear sin" may mean to offer a sacrifice that cancels out the effects of sin or to bear its consequences on behalf of others. The term occurs in John 1:29; 1 John 3:5 (*airō*); and in 1 Peter 2:24 (*anapherō*), citing Isaiah 53: 4 (*pherō*) with 53:12 (*anapherō*).

In the Old Testament, the phrase unequivocally means "to bear guilt," more precisely to bear the punitive consequences of guilt, and in most cases the phrase refers to the bearing of guilt by the person who has sinned (cf. Ezek. 18:20). The possibility of suffering for others is raised by Moses in Exodus 32:30–34, but it is not accepted by God; O. Hofius argues that this is a misunderstanding of a text in which Moses merely declares that if God is going to punish the people, he must punish him along with them. This is not, however, how Paul understands it according to the usual interpretation of Romans 9:3. Following along this line, Hofius further argues that what is in mind in Isaiah 53 is the substitutionary bearing of the consequences of the sin of the many by the Servant, and that *'asham* in Isaiah 53:10 refers to a means of canceling out guilt by bearing the penalty and not to a guilt-offering in the technical sense (as it was understood in the LXX). See "Das vierte Gottesknechtlied in den Briefen des Neuen Testaments." *New Testament Studies* 39 (1993): 414–437.

There are cases where guilty people also incur the punishment for the sins of others (Lam. 5:7; Deut. 5:9). It is doubtful whether these affect the point at issue. In 1 Samuel 15:25, Saul asks Samuel to take away his sin, i.e., presumably to forgive or overlook it (so also in 1 Sam. 25:28). Similarly, God forgives sin (Exod. 34:7). Elsewhere the Israelites bear their sins in the sense of enduring their painful consequences by wandering in

(1 John 2:2; 4:10) and of fellowship with God (i.e., the result of reconciliation). Hebrews develops at full length the concepts of Christ as the sacrifice on the Day of Atonement and as the high priest who puts us in a right relationship with God.

Paul introduces the concept in the context of justification. Justification is a picture drawn from the law court (normally referring to the acquittal of an innocent person or to the release of a person who has personally paid whatever the law requires).[21] For Paul, so far as the guilty are concerned, they do not have to pay anything (Rom. 3:24). This is because something has been done on their behalf. One key passage is Romans 5:8–9 where justification is said to be by Christ's

---

the wilderness for forty years and so atoning for them (Num. 14:34; both *lambanō* and *anapherō* are used in this sense).

Note also the role of the scapegoat which bears the sins of the people (Lev. 16:22). See Williams, G. "The Cross and the Punishment of Sin." In *Where Wrath and Mercy meet: Proclaiming the Atonement Today*, edited by D. Peterson. Carlisle: Paternoster Press, 2001, 68–99.

When the Lamb of God bears sin (John 1:29), this is by making atonement for the sins through sacrificial death. Thus the concepts of dealing with sin by bearing its consequences and by offering sacrifice for it would seem to belong closely together.

J. Jeremias distinguishes the senses of "to take up and carry" and "to carry off", and recognizes that both are possible in John 1:29: either there is a substitutionary bearing of the penalty of sin or there is an expiation for sin (cf. Lev. 10:17). He holds that the former sense is found in Isaiah 53:12 (cf. vs. 4, 6, 11), but prefers the latter sense in John 1:29 because of the reference to the Lamb of God *(TDNT* I: 185–86). To be more precise, Jeremias thinks that originally the saying of John the Baptist referred to Jesus as the Servant of Yahweh who bore the penalty of sin, but in the early church the ambiguous Aramaic *talyā* was understood as "lamb," and the bearing of sin was then understood as the blotting out of sin by the sacrificial efficacy of the blood of Jesus *(TDNT* I: 338–340). Jeremias's *Traditionsgeschichte* has not found scholarly acceptance.

[21] Many scholars have argued for a broader background in God's triumphant restoration of creation and establishment of his rule. While it is true that references to the righteousness of God have a wide Old Testament background, the legal background to the description of the human plight that we have already explored is powerful evidence that the traditional understanding of the language is to be maintained. See Klein, G. "Righteousness in the New Testament." *IDB Sup.*: 750–52.

blood, and we are reminded that while we were sinners Christ died for us. We also need to bear in mind Romans 4:25 where justification is linked to the resurrection of Jesus. But, above all, there is the complex statement in Romans 3:24 which explains that justification takes place by means of the redemption that is in Christ Jesus. The term redemption is used here in the fairly wide sense of deliverance from sin and its consequences. This deliverance is necessary because everyone, whether Jew or Gentiles, is "under sin" (Rom. 3:9). One aspect of this imprisonment under sin is that people are held in the grip of divine judgement (Rom. 3:19). Having explained how redemption is possible, Paul then asserts that God set Christ forth as a *hilastērion* and connects this with a demonstration of his righteousness.

Instead, then, of continuing to explain the grounds for our justification in legal terms, as if justification resulted from something that Jesus did in a law court, like paying the fine for us, or even suffering a death sentence for us, Paul sees Jesus as somehow bringing about redemption and reconciliation with God. This reconciliation (or peace with God, (Rom. 5:1)) is the outcome of whatever is indicated by the term *hilastērion*.

Although not all types of sacrifice were concerned with the problem caused by sin (some were motivated by gratitude and served as means of fellowship with God), there were nevertheless other sacrifices which served to undo the effects of sin not only as regards the land and the people as a whole, but also the individual sinner. The relevant types of Old Testament sacrifices were the sin and burnt offerings and the ritual of the Day of Atonement. This latter included the offering of a goat as a sin offering and the choice of another goat as a scapegoat. Over the scapegoat all the sins of Israel were confessed, and then the goat was sent away into the wilderness where presumably it died. The scapegoat ritual pictured the getting rid of the sin rather than the sinners. The confession of the sin led to the transfer of the sin to the goat. When we read of Christ as the Lamb of God who bears the sins of the world, it is difficult to avoid the impression that the same kind of thing is happening.

The meaning of Paul's key term *hilastērion* is debated. It must refer to a process whereby a rift between God and human beings is removed, where a situation of enmity becomes one of fellowship where people become sons and daughters of God. Practically, this means that God no longer treats transgressors as transgressors because something has happened that makes a different action possible.[22] With due caution we can use the word propitiation,[23] but I shall have something further to say about this. An alternative interpretation of *hilastērion* is to say that something has happened which has the effect of canceling out sin. This might be (in modern terms) the performance of some good deed that makes up for the sin (like restitution being made) or the enactment of a penalty, so that God no longer requires to exclude the sinner. If that is what the word signifies, it is vitally important to recognize that what is happening is that the "mechanism" by which propitiation is effected is being described. That is to say, by adopting a translation like "expiation" for *hilastērion*, we have by no means removed the thought of propitiation from the verse; we are describing what happened, namely expiation for sin, in order that God might be propitiated.

There was an object in the Old Testament cult, the lid of the ark, on which the blood of a sacrifice was smeared annually. This object was referred to in the LXX as the *hilastērion*, the "propitiatory," often paraphrased in English as the mercy-seat. Many commentators argue that this is the source of Paul's rendering here; he is understanding Jesus, more specifically the dying Jesus, as the New Testament counterpart to the lid of the ark smeared with blood, and fulfilling the same function (or rather the function that was symbolized by the lid).[24]

---

[22] This is not the same thing as a change of attitude by God.

[23] So, for example, Wright, N. T. "The Letter to the Romans." *NIB*, X: 4570.

[24] Not to be overlooked is the point explicitly brought out in Hebrews, but implicit elsewhere, that the action involves the offering of the sacrifice to God once the death has taken place. The priest presents the offering to God and, on the strength of it, claims the cancellation of

Further, the same word came into use around the time of Paul to characterize the deaths of Jewish martyrs. In the Books of Maccabees, and specifically in 4 Maccabees, we find an understanding of second-century BC Jewish history which goes like this: Our nation became apostate and disobeyed God, so God judged it by delivering it into the hands of pagan rulers who also persecuted, tortured, and executed those Jews who were actually faithful to God and were thus relatively innocent. While they were dying, they confessed that they were suffering because of the sins of their guilty compatriots, and they pleaded with God to accept their cruel deaths on behalf of the sinful people, and to see in them a sufficient bearing of punishment to enable God to say "the people have suffered enough for their sins at the hands of the pagans, and I will bring it to an end." The writer says: They became, "as it were, a ransom for the sin of our nation. And through the blood of those devout ones and their death as an atoning sacrifice, divine Providence preserved Israel that previously had been mistreated" (4 Macc. 17:22; cf. 12:17 NRSV).[25]

Further illumination comes from the earlier book of 2 Maccabees. Here the martyrs say:

> We are suffering because of our own sins. And if our living God is angry for a little while, to rebuke and discipline us, he will again be reconciled with his own servants… I… give up body and life for the laws of our ancestors, appealing to God to show mercy soon to our nation… and through me and my brothers to bring to an end the wrath of the Almighty that has justly fallen on our whole nation (2 Macc. 7:32-33, 37-38 NRSV).

---

the list of sins held against the people. The sins are expiated and God is appeased in the one action. Hence the sacrifice has been completed and does not need to be repeated or re-enacted. On that objective basis the gospel can be preached. Christ has died: believe the good news.

Other types of sacrifice are also used to explain the death of Jesus. The passover sacrifice (1 Cor. 5:7) and the sin offering both function in this way (Rom. 8:3). Cf. Hooker, *Not Ashamed*, 43–44.

[25] 12:18 in Swete's text.

Both these usages contribute to the background to Paul's statement in Romans 3:25.[26] The former indicates that Jesus' death operates like a sacrifice to restore right relationships between God and sinners. The parallel from 4 Maccabees is particularly important because it refers to suffering and death. In this case, the martyrs do not claim to be sinless, but they are willingly submitting to death. Moreover, the suffering imposed by the pagan ruler is intended by God to rebuke and discipline his people. Although some Jews will die as a result of this suffering, the nation as a whole may be moved to repentance. We must not forget this corporate aspect of biblical thinking, where the suffering and death of some is incidental to the transformation that may come about in the rest of the people as a whole.

If we bear all this in mind, then it becomes clear that Paul is viewing Jesus in his death as functioning in a way that the martyrs only represented partially, and the latter in turn is described in the same way as the annual sacrifice on the Day of Atonement. What has happened is that Paul has interpreted the sin-bearing death of Jesus in terms of the Jewish cult, in the same kind of way as martyrdom was interpreted as sacrificial, and, therefore, there is nothing incongruous about the apparent shift from forensic imagery to sacrificial imagery.

Sacrifice is costly, and it involves the death of a victim. It is made to God. A sacrifice can be understood, in a broad sense, as a penalty, although the specific vocabulary of penalty does not seem to be associated with it. This may indicate that the term penal substitution is too narrow to be applied to every way to understand Christ's death, since we tend to associate the term "penal" with forensic situations and we do not normally think of a sacrifice in forensic terms. It is better to think of a sacrifice as an offering made to God. The fact remains, however, that it is costly and involves the

---

[26] A useful compendium of the background material can be found in Hengel, M. *The Atonement: The Origins of the Doctrine in the New Testament.* London: SCM Press, 1981; cf. "The Expiatory Sacrifice of Christ." *BJRL* 62 (1980): 454–75.

death of a victim who would otherwise have been spared.[27] In his sacrificial death we see God, in the Son, bearing the consequences of our sin so that we do not have to bear them.

Curse

One specific metaphor is that of Christ bearing the curse of the law for sinners (Gal. 3:10–14).

In the Old Testament, God brings the people of Israel into a covenant relationship with him as a result of which blessings and curses rest upon them according to their faithfulness or unfaithfulness to him as regards to giving him exclusive worship and obedience. The sacrificial system is part of this, and is concerned with cleansing the land from the effects of disobedience, and also of restoring individuals to a right relationship with God. In the semi-ideal situation the people maintain their good standing with God by sacrifices despite their sinful lapses. The question of destiny after death hardly arises, since the judgements of God are this-worldly. Nevertheless, basic principles are instantiated which continue to operate after the idea of post-mortem reward and loss comes to the fore.

Those who break the law come under the curse of the law: whoever breaks the law will suffer for so doing. But now, says Paul, Christ has become a curse for us by dying on the cross (Gal. 3:13). Consequently, he has delivered us from the curse. Believers are delivered from the curse of the law by Christ dying on the cross as one accursed. The curse of the law is its condemnation of sinners and statement of judgement over them. The curse cannot simply be laid aside. It is carried out on Christ, and thereby sinners are delivered from it. Again, the one dies for the many, in their place. The principle of one bearing the consequences of sin for the many is present. Here the procedure of the Old Testament criminal law is used to explain Jesus' death, and the element of penalty is conspicuous. This is one of the clearest examples of

---

[27] Cf. G. J. Wenham, "The Theology of Old Testament Sacrifice", in Beckwith and Selman, *Sacrifice*, 75–87.

Christ taking the place of sinners by occupying the accursed position and dying. The law, we remember, is God's law and, therefore, ultimately it is God who imposes the curse. The underlying rationale may well be cultic, in terms of the scapegoat over whom the sins of the people are confessed, and who then wanders off into the wilderness bearing the sins and presumably dies. The thought, however, is transformed by using the language of the curse and applying it to the death of the sinner or the one who bears the sins of others. Although the language of penalty is not used, the thought that Christ endures the consequences of sin and delivers us from having to bear them is clearly expressed.

Redemption and ransom

In this depiction of the state of sinful humanity and its liability to judgement, human beings are under the control of the power of sin (and/or the devil). And the nature of sin is that it kills. Physical death is part of and symbolical of the total death of the sinner. As physical death is exclusion from physical life, so total death is exclusion from spiritual life.

The concept of sin leading to death is fundamental in Paul with his discussion of Adam and the pattern of sin-death that we find there. Here, if anywhere, the concept of sin as a self-destructive force which affects the sinner is present. One might want to ask whether this is incompatible with the more active role of the judge in the forensic metaphor. I see no reason to think so. The way in which sin causes its perpetrators to suffer is certainly part of divine judgement upon it.

Redemption is largely concerned with the delivering of victims of sin from sin, but part of this process is putting them right with God. Hence redemption or deliverance can be equated with the forgiveness of sins (Eph. 1:7). Thus, although we may be redeemed from sin's grasp, the key element is that forgiveness is granted by God. The term forgiveness is appropriate because the sinners do not have to undergo judgement and nothing is required from them by way of condition; so far as they are concerned, redemption is free. But it is made possible through Christ's blood, and, therefore, somehow his death is the means by which it is obtained. Again, we must ask why deliverance from sin and forgiveness are linked to the blood or death of Christ.[28]

Here it is appropriate to mention the passages that use the concept of ransom (Mark 10:45; 1 Tim. 2:6; Titus 2:14) and speak about Christ giving himself or dying to set people free. The root conception of ransom is the making of a payment that sets somebody free, a kind of sale that delivers a person from slavery and bondage. The Old Testament also establishes the practice of redeeming the firstborn (who were supposed to be given to God) by the making of a substitute offering (Exod. 13:11–16; 34:19–20).[29] The price is a substitute for the person redeemed, and in that the price is costly it is, we might say, painful. Hence the concept of substitution is present and the cost may be regarded as a penalty in the broad sense. This is manifestly the case where it is the precious blood of Christ that brings about people's redemption. Consequently, the principle of penal substitution can be seen to be effective here. A ransom need not imply substitution of one person for another. It may simply be a monetary payment. Peter, however, makes the point that we were ransomed with blood (cf. 1 Pet. 1:18–19). There is the clear implication that the price is of infinite worth so that it avails for all people; the principle that the death of this particular One is able to ransom many sinners is manifest. Since, as we have seen, death is the ultimate consequence of sin, and Christ suffered death, it would seem to me to require special pleading to argue that his death was anything other than a bearing of the death that sin inflicts upon sinners so that they might not have to bear it.

---

[28] The blood is not mentioned in the parallel passage in Colossians 1:14, except in some late MSS that have harmonized the text to that of Ephesians; but one has not to read very far to find mention of it in connection with the reconciliation of God's enemies (Col. 1:20).

[29] A special case is the Passover. God passed over the houses where the blood showed that a lamb had been slain (although, in this case, such elements as the offering of the lamb to God are absent). The first-born does not die. This apotropaic ritual would seem to be redemptive.

Reconciliation

The situation presupposed by the use of this language is that
there is enmity between God and the unreconciled, a mutual
enmity as we have seen. God reckons the sins of people
against them and they are his enemies. The concept of wrath
expresses the personal reaction of God to his enemies. When
sinners rebel against God, the consequence is that he excludes
them from fellowship with him. The biblical idea of wrath
is closely linked to judgement, and it expresses more the
reaction of God when the justice and mercy that he wants to
see is replaced by injustice and hatred. Nevertheless, wrath
is also a concept which is equally at home in this sphere of
discourse. And, in fact, it is hard to separate them rigidly in
the Bible. It is natural that those who rebel against God and
will not abandon their rebellion should be excluded from the
community that they are disrupting. They are excluded from
God's favor.

Romans 5:9–11 makes it plain that reconciliation takes
place by the death of Christ. In 2 Corinthians 5:18–21, Christ's
function is to be made sin on behalf of the sinners, and, in
this same context, there is reference to his death on behalf
of all. The rationale is not explained. Some scholars see here
simply an exchange: he became what we are in order that
we might become what he is. But this leaves unexplained
what actually happens. To put it plainly, what happens to
the sin that is taken by Christ? Somehow it must be taken
away, and this could not happen without his death. But
Christ became sin for sinners and died for them (note the
inescapable connection of 2 Cor. 5:14–15 and 19–21 which
makes it clear that Christ becoming sin and Christ dying are
inseparable from each other). The implication is that somehow
this took away their sin and liability to judgement/wrath,
so that they might enjoy the status of righteousness which
is possible because God no longer holds their sins against
them. The consequences of sin, specifically death, are borne
by Christ when he is made one with sinners, and, in that
sense, the substitution is penal. Sinners are invited to receive
the reconciliation that has been objectively achieved.

Forgiveness

Closely linked with reconciliation is the concept of forgiveness. The essence of human forgiveness is that an offence is wiped away without the imposition of a penalty or with mitigation of the penalty. Forgiveness is usually an offer to restore good relationships between the victim and the offender, in which the victim no longer holds the offence against the offender, without requiring any restitution or punishment. The offended person is prepared to overlook the fault and enter into a positive relationship with the offender.

Are there any conditions attached? In human personal relationships, an expression of contriteness by the offender is often seen by the offended person as sufficient ground for forgiveness. Even in a forensic situation, the presence or absence of contrition may have some effect upon the judge's act of sentencing. But there is a distinction between an offer of forgiveness and the willingness to accept it, and, if the reception of forgiveness is not accompanied by contrition and repentance on the part of the offender, nothing is achieved.

In biblical and Jewish thought, great importance is attached to repentance or penitence as an essential factor if forgiveness is to be offered to an offender. Some expression of regret is important, and, needless to say, this regret should come from the heart and not be merely an empty form of words if it is to be acceptable to God and, indeed, to the community. Forgiveness, then, may be conditional on the expression of penitence by the offender, but in ordinary usage it certainly is not something that is offered after punishment has been exacted.

In the human sphere, forgiveness is not always appropriate. In the case of children, parents may have to exercise sanctions lest the children think that they can offend as much as they like and get away with it. There is a process of moral education to be undertaken. Equally a criminal justice system cannot work on this principle or else crime would multiply without restraint. But, in both of these cases, it is the undesirable effects of free forgiveness on the offenders that are the problem.

The usual human understanding of forgiveness excludes the possibility that people who forgive must first exercise some kind of retribution before they can forgive. The legal official doesn't say to the person who has just paid a fine: "And now I forgive you," although, of course, once the fine has been paid, the original situation before the offence has been restored and the offence is no longer held against the person. This suggests that there is some distinction in ordinary usage between forgiveness, where no restitution or retribution is required, and the situation where an act of restitution or retribution is required and only after it has been carried out is the offence no longer held against the person. Human forgiveness thus involves some kind of cost borne by the forgiver who does not require whatever restitution might be thought appropriate and foregoes the element of retribution that is necessary for the upholding of righteousness and justice. The offender does not have to undergo some painful penalty. And this would seem to be the kind of forgiveness that Jesus told his disciples to practice.

When the New Testament speaks of divine forgiveness, we have to understand it as requiring no restitution or retribution from the sinner, but as resting on something that God in his mercy has done to make it possible. It certainly needs to be accepted by the sinner, and some change in the sinner is involved in the process. Although such an offer is made, the offender may not be contrite, and sin's grip is such that sinners are not capable of showing the necessary contrition. Old Testament sacrifices could be understood as expressions of contrition, with the offering of a (valuable) article as expression and proof of the inner feeling. These were offered in accordance with a divine direction that this way of dealing with sin was prescribed by God and acceptable to him. The sins in question were publicly confessed: the sinners laid hands on the sacrifice to indicate that it was their sacrifice and was in respect of the actual sins confessed. In this way the sacrifice could be said to take away sin.

In the New Testament, the danger of thinking that an outward act can deal with sin is clearly recognized (Heb. 10:4, 11). God, who provided the path of sacrifice in the Old

Testament, now intervenes to provide a new offering, himself dying in the person of the Son who has united himself with humanity. This is the offering which will deal with sin. Christ, or his name or his death, are integral to the New Testament concept of forgiveness.[30] In Hebrews, forgiveness is seen as the fruit of sacrifice (Heb. 9:22; 10:18). In Ephesians 1:7, it is linked to Jesus' blood. In Colossians 1:14, it is not far distant from a reference to peace being made by the blood of the cross (Col. 1:20). Thus God takes the initiative, God himself bears the sin and gives his Son in his sacrificial death as the way or means by which sinners can come to him. The sinner no longer needs to bring an offering to God, for Christ has already made that offering in the heavenly sanctuary. The conferral of forgiveness costs the sinner nothing, but it costs God everything.

Again, then, in the broad sense we may see the consequences of our sin painfully borne by God himself in the Son, a sacrificial death taking place whereby we are saved.

Conclusion

From this survey it is clear that essentially the same basic principle is expressed in each of these different understandings of the death of Jesus. The principle of one person bearing the painful consequences of sin is the *modus operandi* of the different understandings of the cross. This is perhaps not surprising when one considers how the New Testament writers can intertwine the different metaphors so readily.

I conclude that the metaphors belong together and are used side by side, and, to a great extent, express a situation in which the same structure can be perceived. There are different nuances in these expressions of the nature of salvation, but the central action can be regarded as God doing something in Christ that involves Christ's death while bearing our sins. This is the painful consequence of our sins, and it saves us from that painful consequence of exclusion from the kingdom

---

[30] Forgiveness is expressly linked to Christ, his name or his death in Matthew 26:28; Acts 2:38; 5:31; 10:43; 13:38; 24:47; Ephesians 1:7; Colossians 1:14; Hebrews 9:22; 1 John 1:9; 2:12.

of God. These points seem to me to be common to all these understandings of the cross. Thus the term penal substitution can be appropriately used of it, although we might possibly improve our language somewhat.

We thus have an understanding of the death of Christ as the means provided by God to take away human sin and its penalty. It is an action with which sinners can identify themselves. The death of Christ is the death of the sinners who accept what he has done on their behalf and instead of them, and yet may be said to identify themselves with it. They can reckon themselves to have died to sin.[31]

An angry and violent God?

If we have come this far, I believe that we have laid an adequate foundation to rebut the objections that centre on the accusation that the Bible depicts an angry and violent God. Specific accusations include such statements as these:

> The imagery depicts an angry Father who is persuaded to show mercy by the Son.
> There is a conflict between mercy and justice/judgement in God.
> The Father demands human sacrifice before he can forgive.
> The Father inflicts violence on the Son.[32]

---

[31] I have discussed the way in which the substitution of Christ for the sinner leads to the identification of the believer with him in *New Testament Theology*. Downers Grove: IVP/Leicester: Apollos, 2004, 223–226. For a fuller and deeper discussion see Denney, J. *The Death of Christ*, edited by R. V. G. Tasker. London: Tyndale Press, 1951; reprinted Carlisle: Paternoster Press, 1997.

[32] It is sometimes alleged that the doctrine of penal substitution effectively dates from the Reformation and was virtually absent or unformulated earlier. However, a distinction must be made between the existence of the doctrine and the degree of use made of it. The doctrine of penal substitution may not be prominent before the Reformation, but this is quite different from saying that it was unknown. Thus, while Green and Baker, *Recovering*, 119–21, can show how great stress is laid on the doctrine of recapitulation in Irenaeus, they also rightly point out that Irenaeus includes statements of propitiation. Irenaeus, like other early Christian theologians, is concerned both with the deliverance of sinners from their sin and also

These criticisms need to be answered, and I believe that the way to do so is not by denying the biblical perception of the significance of the death of Jesus, but by understanding it correctly.[33]

---

with the mending of their relationship with God. Similarly, Blocher gathers together patristic and other pre-Reformation statements which show that the doctrine was certainly held but was not central (Blocher, "Biblical Metaphors," 630-631). Further evidence from Origen, Cyril of Alexandria and Augustine is supplied by Boersma (Boersma, *Violence*, 158–163). If the doctrine was not central in patristic and medieval theology, then that maybe belongs with the general tendency to misunderstand the grace of God that T. F. Torrance rightly detected as occurring from an early stage, and that was not put right until the Reformers brought the church back to the New Testament. See Torrance, T. F. *The Doctrine of Grace in the Apostolic Fathers*. Edinburgh: Oliver and Boyd, 1948.

[33] It may be helpful at this point to gather together in more detail some comments on the case against penal substitution mounted by Green and Baker, *Recovering*.

1. It ignores or sidesteps the New Testament teaching on wrath and judgement. It ignores the full extent of the evidence in the Synoptic Gospels, specifically the sayings about baptism and the cup, the latter of which is to be understood in terms of the metaphor of drinking the cup of God's wrath. The theology implicit in the baptism statement and the ransom statement is not explored.

It caricatures the understanding of wrath in terms of arbitrary, violent emotion. It claims that wrath is not a divine property or essential attribute. Certainly it is "the divine response to human unfaithfulness," but it is [merely] "God's letting us go our own way" (55). Thus the fact of divine wrath is not denied, but it is not something that God feels (like he presumably feels love). Paul is said to lack "any developed sense of divine retribution." All this is stated rather than defended.

2. The sacrificial language of the New Testament is largely set aside and its implications ignored. Although the importance of sacrifice and bearing the curse in Paul is recognized, the authors play down the significance of the former by arguing that there were various types of sacrifice and not all were concerned with the removal of sin. But this does not affect the basic point that some of them were concerned with sin, and many required the blood that made atonement. Again, the fact of vicarious substitution is recognized, but it is stated that God does not need to be appeased; rather he acts to bring humanity back to himself (59). Here there is some inconsistency in that the authors allow the teaching in Galatians 3 full force: Jesus bears the curse of God on our behalf. If that is not penal substitution I do not know what it is. Again, the function of the death of Christ in terms of the mercy seat is acknowledged (63), but little attempt

It is easy for opponents of penal substitution to present the matter as though it is only because of the cross that God is prepared to abandon his wrath and forgive sinners. Certainly this is a frequent criticism of the doctrine. Yet I am not aware that any responsible defenders of the doctrine take this point of view, and if there were, I would side with their critics.[34]

---

is made to understand it. It would seem that time and again this book recognizes the existence of evidence for the position that is being opposed but quite fails to attempt to explain it away; it just ignores it.

Similarly, the possibility of an atonement theology that starts from the Passover as an atoning sacrifice in John is ignored. It is assumed that the *hilasmos* teaching in 1 John can be neutralized by concentrating on the imagery of the scapegoat which banishes the people's sins without a sacrifice or appeasing God. And, although the presence of sacrificial teaching in Hebrews is acknowledged and the phrase 'expiatory sacrifice' is used, there is no real discussion of the way in which this evidence is a major obstacle to the proposed thesis.

The one major point that might be raised in favor of the Green and Baker approach is the lack of atonement language in Acts. Salvation is understood as status-reversal, but what makes status-reversal possible is not discussed. Obviously the gospel can be proclaimed without enunciating a theology of atonement, but what we are concerned with here is the theology on which the gospel rests. For example, I suppose that you could preach the gospel to Gentiles without mentioning the fact that the death of Christ took place according to the Scriptures, although that element would be important in preaching to Jews. The fact that Paul can express a theology of conversion that refers only to the resurrection of Jesus and confession of faith in him as Lord in Romans 10 does not imply that he has forgotten all that he said in the earlier chapters of the letter! The absence of atonement from some evangelistic sermons does not mean that it is a dispensable part of Christian theology. Our concern here is with the theology that must underlie the preaching of the gospel, rather than with the specific forms that this preaching may take with different audiences.

I have to conclude that this book just does not establish the proposition that it puts forward by showing how the texts claimed to support it actually do so and by responding adequately to the texts that offer prima facie evidence against it. The result is that the denial of penal substitution is in danger of being seen as a simple denial of what Scripture says rather than (as the authors would presumably wish) as a convincing re-interpretation of what Scripture does say.

[34] A study of Edwards D. L., and J. Stott. *Essentials: A liberal-evangelical dialogue*. London: Hodder & Stoughton, 1988, 107–168, will make the point absolutely clear.

The divine initiative

I start with the fact that biblical thinking contains paradoxes and tensions that may relativize some statements. Two examples must suffice. One is the situation of slaves and free persons. In 1 Corinthians 7:21–24, Paul says that human slaves who have become God's people are freed people,[35] belonging to Jesus; but then he also says that other people who were humanly free become slaves of Christ. Putting these two statements together we must conclude that all believers are, in one sense, slaves and, in another, free.[36] Alongside this is the way in which the disciples in John's Gospel who acknowledge Jesus as their Lord are told that they are not his slaves but his friends (John 15:15), and Paul makes the point that believers are no longer slaves but sons (Gal. 4:7). Must we not say that the less personal relationships are somehow redefined and sublimated by being taken up into the more personal ones?

A second, more controversial, example is the language of mutual service and subjection in Paul's letters (Gal. 5:13; Eph. 5:21; Phil. 2:1–4; cf. John 13:14), which probably implies that the so-called subjection in marriage is not one-sided but mutual. So statements that appear to be in tension with one another if taken absolutely have to be understood at a deeper level.

But these are simply illustrations to prepare the way for another point. It is absolutely fundamental in the New Testament that it is God the Father who personally initiates and acts in the coming and death of Jesus to bring about redemption. The motive for the death of Jesus is stated to be the loving purpose of God, and there is not the faintest hint in the New Testament that Jesus died to persuade God to forgive sinners. On the contrary, his death is part of the way in which God himself acts in his grace and mercy.

There is a possible objection to these assertions. It is strange that we are told that the Son and the Spirit both intercede for believers with the Father, as if he needed to be persuaded to

---

[35] Strictly they are "freed" people of the Lord, not "free."
[36] Cf. Romans 1:1; 1 Corinthians 6:19–20; Galatians 5:1, 13.

forgive (Rom. 8:27, 34; Heb. 7:25; 1 John 2:1). However, in the same breath, Paul assures us that God knows the mind of the Spirit, that the Spirit intercedes according to the will of God and that the God to whom the Son intercedes is for us, gave up his Son for us and will reject anybody who brings a charge against us, his elect. These passages make it abundantly clear to me that the picture of intercession must be understood as a figure of speech from human relationships that must not be pressed too far to imply that the Father's mind is different from that of the Son or of the Spirit. There is no way in which this picture can be understood in terms of a difference of purpose between Father and Son. The picture of intercession is a condescension to human beings who might think of God as other than the Jesus whom they know as the friend of sinners and assures them that the Father is in agreement with him. The statement about Christ's intercession in Romans 8 comes in the context of the extraordinarily powerful statements of the love of God the Father shown to us in the death of his Son.

We have a more clearly formulated doctrine of the Trinity now than was possible for the first Christians in the infancy of Christian theologizing, and we can understand perhaps more fully how the Father, Son, and Spirit are bound together in a fellowship of love so that they have the same purposes and the same knowledge. Therefore, the picture of intercession is simply one way of assuring us that the Father shares the same loving purpose for us as the Jesus whom we know to have died for us and who is now in heaven with the Father, and as the Spirit who dwells in us and assures us of the love of God in our hearts and who speaks directly to the Father in heaven. There is an indissoluble unity between Father, Son, and Spirit in the work of redemption.[37] The recognition that it is God the Son, that is to say quite simply God, who suffers and dies on the cross, settles the question finally. This is God himself bearing the consequences of sin, not the abuse of some cosmic child.

---

[37] This is one of the pieces of evidence that lead to the principle *opera Trinitatis ad extra sunt indivisa*; cf. Heppe, H. *Reformed Dogmatics*. London: George Allen and Unwin, 1950, 116.

The God who suffers

We can go further. The death of Jesus is the single action of Father and Son together. We can only think of them in human terms: the Father sends the Son; the Son obeys the Father and becomes incarnate; the Son dies on the cross. Nevertheless, the Father is in Christ reconciling the world to himself. We may debate whether this critical verse means that the Father was, as it were, in Christ or that the Father was reconciling the world through the agency of Christ. Perhaps both ideas are present.[38]

But, once we have said this, we have eliminated any understanding of the cross which depicts the Son satisfying the claims of the Father and persuading the Father to do what he did not want to do. Instead, we have moved to the reality of the Father himself giving his Son for us. Some theologians have speculated on the anguish of the Father himself enduring separation from the One who calls out, "Why have you forsaken me?" Indeed, there are mysteries here that we cannot fathom. God the Father is there at the cross, self-sacrificially giving his Son to be one with humanity and die for its sins, and somehow there is a separation as the Son does what human beings cannot do: he bears their sins. Paradoxically God is both present and absent. The Bible shows Jesus not just as a representative, substitutionary man bearing the sins of the world, but as God, God the Son, God in Christ, taking on himself the sin of the world and its consequences, and enduring them in himself to deliver us from them. "Tis mystery all, the immortal dies." "Faith cries out, "Tis he, 'Tis he, my God who suffers there!"" (C. Wesley).[39]

In the last analysis we cannot separate the operations of the Trinity and have the members of the Godhead working

[38] Harris, M. J. *The Second Epistle to the Corinthians.* Grand Rapid, MI: Eerdmans/Milton Keynes: Paternoster Press, 2005, 440–43, argues that Paul is referring to "God's being present and active in Christ through whom he (God) effected reconciliation." Nor should the role of the Holy Spirit in the sacrifice of Christ (Heb. 9:14) be overlooked.

[39] I am aware that there are problems with the issue of divine passivity or impassivity, and regret that I have not been able to take them up here.

independently or in any kind of tension with one another, nor can we separate the divine and the human in Christ.

At the cross, then, it is God himself suffering with, and on behalf of, human beings. There is a hint of this in the Old Testament where we may pick up the deep insight of Isaiah 63:9, which tells us that when Israel was afflicted by its enemies: "In all their distress he too was distressed, and the angel of his presence saved them," and yet the very next verse has to say: "they rebelled and grieved his Holy Spirit. So he turned and became their enemy and he himself fought against them" (Isa. 63:10). Here is the paradoxical (to us) recognition of God as Savior and Judge.

It could be argued, as some theologians do, that all God needs to do in regard to sinners is to uphold justice, and that he has no duty to them beyond that. They have no claims on his mercy. Yet, while James tells us: "Judgment without mercy will be shown to anyone who has not been merciful." He then adds: "Mercy triumphs over judgment" (Jas. 2:13). That principle must surely be true of God himself, and it reminds us that beyond justice lies the mercy of God, which goes beyond justice, in the narrow sense, to deliver people who have come under judgement. James Torrance used to remind us that God could not give Christians the command to love their enemies if he himself did not do so.

God provides the means of atonement

The crucial and startling consequence is that Jesus does not propitiate the Father so as to change his attitude to sinners and make it possible for him to forgive sin. Rather, Father and Son together take upon themselves all the suffering and judgement caused by and due to sin, and bear them for us. If Jesus Christ the Son is God, just as God the Father is God, then there can be no sense in which God propitiates God, any more than God needs to intercede with God. But both types of statement are intended to indicate as powerfully as possible that God is on our side to deliver us from our sins and their consequences. The language of propitiation is thus on the same level as the language of intercession, where the God who is propitiated and the God who responds to intercession is the God who initiates and carries out the self-propitiation (if we may so call it) and the self-intercession.

This is no new conclusion. We are back with one of the greatest modern expositors of the evangelical doctrine of the cross, James Denney, who wrote: "I have often wondered whether we might not say that the Christian doctrine of the Atonement just meant that in Christ God took the responsibility of evil upon Himself and somehow subsumed evil under good."[40] I would only comment that I am suspicious of sayings with "just" in them lest they be over-simplifications, and I reckon that Denney would agree that that simple statement, in fact, would need a lot of unpacking. But, if we want a simple statement that expresses the heart of the atonement, it would be difficult to better this one.

Might we say that, from a human angle, Jesus provides in his death the offering that we as sinners need if we are to be reconciled to God, but that, from the divine point of view, what we see is Father and Son united in love and righteousness to save sinners? Consequently, the action of Jesus does not propitiate God in order to make him willing to forgive, but rather provides the means by which God deals with the sin that forms a barrier between himself and sinners. It does not, of course, merely give them peace of mind and reassurance that God is willing to receive them, though that is not unimportant, but, far more importantly, it creates the path whereby forgiveness is possible, "Pardon – from an offended God!" (S. Davies).

The death of Jesus is not a means of appeasing a Father who is unable or unwilling to forgive. It is the divinely

---

[40] From a letter to P. C. Simpson written in 1915; Denney, J. *Letters of Principal James Denney to His Family and Friends*. London, 1921, 187.

God "wills that sin shall be punished, but He does not will that sin shall be punished without also willing that the punishment shall fall on Himself" (Hodgson, *Doctrine*, 77); this is a clear statement of penal substitution, but later Hodgson refers to Quick's distinction between penal and sacrificial death (*Doctrine*, 148); Quick himself, however, was not happy with the notion of penal substitution; see Quick, O. C. *Doctrines of the Creed: Their Basis in Scripture and Their Meaning Today*. London: Nisbet, 1938, 228–231.

appointed way by which sinners, who would otherwise
face the wrath and judgement of God, can approach him
and claim his mercy on the grounds that Christ bore that
judgement by dying for them. The basis for the gospel for
sinners is what God has already done for them; it is because
the reconciliation has already been made that sinners are
urged to accept what God has done for them.[41]

Judgement and mercy

It may be that behind some of the criticism lies an unwilling-
ness to recognize the fact of a divine judgement that must
be taken seriously. Judgement is necessary, at the very least,
to discourage sinners from sin,[42] but we have seen that it
is the inevitable consequence of the holy love that God has

---

[41] The case against propitiation and penal substitution is put with care
by Smail, *Once and For All*, 80–99. The problems that he sees include the
oddity of saying that God propitiated himself, the way in which to speak
of propitiation so readily suggests the idea that God had to be persuaded
to forgive, and the suggestion that Christ was punished instead of sinners.
These points raise the question whether the use of this language almost
inevitably leads to misunderstanding. Smail wants to say that Christ
entered into the just consequences of our sinning, and to see salvation
being effected more by his vicarious obedience, as part of which he bears
the judgement of our sins.

Christ's active obedience is certainly a vital part of his saving work, but
recognition of it need not lead to a denial of his bearing of judgement and
the making of a sacrifice. And the propitiation or atonement made by God
himself is the deepest expression of his love. "So far from finding any kind
of contrast between love and propitiation, the apostle can convey no idea
of love to anyone except by pointing to the propitiation – love is what is
manifested there; and he can give no account of the propitiation but by
saying, 'Behold what manner of love'" (Denney, J. *The Death of Christ*, 152).
That is the paradox that we dare not explain away.

[42] It has been argued that the warning passages addressed to believers in
Hebrews and elsewhere have the function of encouraging sinful believers
not to apostatize, and they function so effectively that, in fact, no sinful
believers will ever apostatize, and the judgement described can thus be
said to be hypothetical in that nobody will actually suffer it. Cf. Schreiner
T. R., and A. B. Caneday. *The Race Set Before Us: A Biblical Theology of
Perseverance and Assurance*. Downers Grove: IVP, 2001, 163. Whatever our
assessment of this proposal, in the present case the judgement is real and
not hypothetical.

for his creation. Therefore, there can be no suggestion that divine judgement is not a reality.[43] God's judgement upon sin is the abandoning of sinners to a situation without him, so that they are left under the power of sin and false gods that cannot save, and the end result is death. That is the nature of judgement, in that God wills it to be so. It leaves sinners to their sin. And God so wills it in order that his kingdom may be seen to repudiate sin and the sinners who do not repent of their sin.

In the light of these considerations, I would argue that the accusations made against penal substitution can be answered.

The Father is not persuaded to show mercy by the Son; rather, the Father sent the Son and they act together. There is no conflict between justice and mercy. The Father is dealing with the mystery of evil and its consequences to deliver sinners. The death of Jesus is not a human sacrifice to enable God to forgive, but the action of God himself who, in his mercy, provides the remedy for sin: it cannot be too strongly emphasized that it is God who suffers on the cross.

And the Father does not inflict violence on the Son; rather, the Son who is God takes upon himself the consequences of cosmic and human sin and defeats them. The Son takes death upon himself freely and voluntarily in obedience to the Father, and the Father, for his part, overcomes death by raising the Son from the dead. What God in Christ does is to enter into this violent world and defeat it precisely by non-violence, as Peter points out so carefully in 1 Peter 2:21–25. If the Son is non-violent, we can hardly say that, in contrast to him, the Father is violent.

It is inherent in this understanding that the death of Christ is not the event that persuades God, otherwise unwilling, to forgive; it is not the event that makes him willing. Rather, (1)

---

[43] I sometimes think that the critics of divine judgement want to have it both ways. On the one hand, they insist that God, as the moral ruler of the world, is against the evil that is present in it, speaks out through his prophets in condemnation of it, and wants to overthrow it. On the other hand, they don't allow him to act in judgement and actually to pull down the mighty from their thrones.

the death is purposed and initiated by God himself; (2) the death is the death of God himself, since the Son is one with the Father, and we are correct to see God dying on the cross, as Charles Wesley's hymns clearly teach. The death is God identifying with humanity in its need, and this is important in showing how God in Christ absorbs the suffering that evil and sinners inflicted on humanity (not only the cruelty of the executioners and the taunts of the bystanders, but also the actual pain of dying that is part of the corruption produced by cosmic evil). Some scholars complain that the idea of "absorption" is unbiblical;[44] I cannot see that this objection is justified, since we have to use terms that do not occur in the Bible in order to bring out its teaching. The Bible talks clearly enough about God's bearing sin, and that is an adequate basis for this language of absorption, which means that God takes upon himself our sin and bears its consequences so that we do not have to bear them.

The charge of cosmic child abuse is totally misplaced. It fails to recognize the points that have just been made which emphasize that it was God who initiated the cross, it was God himself who suffered on the cross and bore the sin of the world. A parent who puts herself into the breach and dies to save her child from a burning house is considered praiseworthy. The God who suffers and dies in the person of Jesus for human sin belongs in the same category. It is true that the concept of God the Son suffering and dying is paradoxical and incomprehensible, and we have to recognize that fact, but that is what Scripture says. It is part of the mystery of the incarnation.[45]

---

[44] Blocher, "Biblical Metaphors," 643.

[45] There is a criticism of a quite different sort which needs to be mentioned. Despite such statements in classical documents as that Christ "made a full perfect and sufficient oblation for the sins of the whole world" (*Book of Common Prayer*), and the clear declaration of the New Testament that "Christ gave himself as a ransom for all people" (1 Tim. 2:6), there have been some attempts to tie the doctrine of penal substitution to a doctrine of limited or particular atonement; some scholars hold that penal substitution can be defended only on the basis that Christ acts as substitute only for those who are actually saved by this death rather than being a saviour who makes an atoning sacrifice for the sins of the whole world (1 John 2:2)

It is, then, not a case of God being angry with Christ but of God himself in Christ taking on himself sin and its penalty. Indeed, at some point the challenge needs to be issued: where are these evangelicals who say that God was angry with Christ? Name them![46] Where are the evangelicals who will repudiate this statement: "We do not, however, insinuate that God was ever hostile to him or angry with him," written by John Calvin?[47] You will not find them among serious theologians, although I recognize that popular preachers may err in this respect. And it does seem to be the case that much

---

in accordance with the desire of God that all might be saved (John 3:16; 1 Tim. 2:4–6; 2 Pet. 3:9). Otherwise, it is argued, in the case of those who are not saved, God would have demanded the penalty twice, once from Christ and once from themselves when they suffer the penalty of disobedience. Cf. Jeffery, S., M. Ovey and A. Sach. *Pierced for our Transgressions: Rediscovering the glory of penal substitution.* Nottingham: IVP, 2007, 268–78.

However this objection is without any force because it assumes a kind of mathematical equivalence between the death of Christ and the penalty due to sinners; there is nothing unjust about penalizing offenders who refuse to accept the offer of an amnesty. Those of us who were brought up on Hammond, T. C. *In Understanding be Men.* London: Inter-Varsity Fellowship, 1938[3], 159, were forewarned against that misapprehension. The doctrine of penal substitution is not part of a package which also contains as essential the concepts of particular election and limited (or definite) atonement. "None need perish; all may live, for Christ has died" (Sanders, W. In *The Methodist Hymnbook* [London: Methodist Conference Office, 1933], No. 315). Sadly, however, it is not inevitable that all will respond positively when the gospel news is sounding.

[46] Guillebaud, H. E. *Why the Cross?* London: Inter-Varsity Fellowship, 1946[2], 145, explicitly repudiates the phrase "God punished Christ." Similarly, Stott, *Cross*, 150–151.

Admittedly Grudem, W. *Systematic Theology.* Leicester: IVP/Grand Rapids, MI: Zondervan, 1994, 575, can say that "God... poured out on Jesus the fury of his wrath: Jesus became the object of the intense hatred of sin and vengeance against sin which God had patiently stored up since the beginning of the world." One can see how such language can be misunderstood.

[47] Calvin, J. *Institutes of the Christian Religion* 2:16:11, translated by H. Beveridge. London: J. Clarke, 1953, I, 444. A. T. B. McGowan (to whom I am indebted for several helpful comments) explains that Calvin affirmed that God punished Jesus instead of us but denied that the Father was angry with the Son. Travis and others hold that Christ endured God's judgement on sin but did not suffer God's punishment for sin.

of the criticism comes from the more radical feminist type of theologian with an agenda that includes repudiation of essential features of biblical theology.

Conclusion

What exactly have we achieved in this examination of the subject?[48] I suggest that we have done four things.

First, we began by examining the New Testament evidence, principally in Paul but backed up and confirmed by the other writers. Various imagery is used for the significance of Christ's death. We have seen especially how Christ has taken upon himself the sin of humanity, and the suffering and death resulting from it. This led us to explore more fully the nature of judgement upon wrongdoing and sin. I have tried to show that judgement has various connected functions. These include the expression of the rejection of sin and unrepentant sinners by God and his people, and the provision of an offering of the repentance and restitution that sinners ought to (but

---

[48] These are not the only problems that critics have raised with regard to the doctrine of substitution. Another set of questions concerns the danger that if Christ acts as substitute for us and we have nothing to do except have faith, then there is the danger that there may be no real change in us. We cheerfully accept what somebody else has done for us but it doesn't necessarily change us into different people. Within the scope of the present discussion there is no room to take up this theme. All that I can briefly say is that this objection does not take into account the way in which Paul in particular develops his doctrine of faith-union with Christ in his death, burial and resurrection so that our life takes on the same cruciform shape. There is thus a kind of reverse action, whereby, delivered from death as the wages of sin, we die with Christ to sinful desires and sin. The criticism entirely ignores the motive of gratitude that is aroused by so great a sacrifice: we love, because he first loved us. It fails to reckon with the fact that faith is an act of commitment to Jesus, resulting in a transfer of ownership from sin to our risen Lord; the basic Christian confession is "Jesus is Lord" rather than "Jesus is Savior." Nor can conversion be separated from all that is associated with new birth and indwelling by Spirit through which the risen life of Christ becomes a reality in us. The objection is totally unjustified. See my *New Testament Theology: Many Witnesses, One Gospel*. Downers Grove: IVP/Leicester: Apollos, 2004, 223–226.

cannot) offer. Jesus, as the sinless Man and as the Son of God, becomes one with sinners in their sin; in his own person, he not only shows the perfect righteousness and obedience to God that they failed to show, but also, and above all, he bears their sin and all its consequences so as to overcome the power of sin and to express the divine disapproval of it. He undoubtedly acts in the place of sinners, and he undoubtedly suffers the consequences of their sin. Therefore, we rightly call his act substitutionary.[49] If we broaden out the sense of the term "penal" to embrace all those consequences in which he not only suffers the pain inflicted by hostile sinners upon other people, including God himself, but also the pain that comes upon sinners themselves, then it seems to me that the continued use of the term is fully justified. So I am suggesting, first, that a clarification of the nature of judgement helps us to a better understanding of the death of Christ.

However, second, if the phrase arouses wrong ideas of God inflicting violent pain upon his Son, then we should be prepared to adopt another term that is less open to misunderstanding.[50] "Substitutionary suffering and death"

---

[49] The concept of "representative" is sometimes used instead, but it risks conveying only the idea of one person acting on behalf of and representing humanity, which is true as far as it goes, but does not bring out adequately the crucial fact that it is the Son of God who takes on this role and does instead of human beings what they cannot do. Once we say that Christ, as the Son of God, does something instead of us, we are talking of substitution.

[50] Denney refers to death as the judgement upon sin rather than as the penalty. Interestingly the term "penal substitution" does not appear to have been used in his writings, although he certainly used the term "substitution." J. M. Gordon says (personal communication) that "he uses the words 'penal' and 'substitute' but keeps them apart, preferring phrases like 'the divine condemnation.'" The point was already noted by Packer, "What did the cross achieve?", 28, who noted how the substance of the idea was expressed by Denney in other terms. Cf. *The Death of Christ*, 103, for as strong a statement as any. Denney insisted that Christ bore the condemnation due to our sin (e.g., *Studies in Theology*. London: Hodder and Stoughton, 1899, 108). "The sin is laid by God on the Sinless One; its doom is laid on Him; His death is the execution of the divine sentence upon it" (*The Second Epistle to the Corinthians*. London: Hodder and Stoughton, 1907, 220). Packer himself has no problem about using the phrase; see "What did the cross achieve?"

will do very well, although it is more cumbersome. We may compare how, although the term "fundamentalist" has a noble ancestry, nevertheless, it has been so twisted in popular usage that it is not helpful for us to use it of ourselves, however much we hold fast to those fundamental doctrines that were upheld by our forerunners. That is to say, concepts, and the phraseology used to express them, are distinguishable, and it is possible for us to hold fast to the concept of penal substitution while looking for terminology that may communicate it more effectively to our contemporaries.

The third thing that we have done is to recognize the importance of Trinitarian thinking in relation to the death of Jesus Christ, the Son of God, This enables us to take seriously the fact that the Father and the Son are acting together in the act of atonement; God bears in himself the dire consequences of sin so that sinners, who are totally unable to save themselves, may be delivered from their sin through faith in the Son of God who loved them and gave himself for them (Gal. 2:20). and the God who demonstrates his own love toward them in that Christ died for them (Rom. 5:8). The doctrine of the Trinity is our firm defense against any false suggestion that God the Father had to be appeased by the Son in order to bring about his purpose of redemption.

Fourth, and finally, I believe that in such ways as these, we can both clarify and defend the doctrine expressed in the phrase "penal substitution," and I shall continue to subscribe to declarations of the evangelical faith that enshrine this fundamental and essential doctrine and to sing with reverent thanksgiving and praise:

T. C. Hammond comments: "The terms which are used in reproach of this doctrine, such as 'the penal view', are in themselves too ambiguous to clarify the issues on the subject, and frequently reveal a misunderstanding of what is being suggested by those who believe in propitiation" (*In Understanding*, 149; cf. 159). Nevertheless, he did write of "Penal Suffering." "In the sense of His taking upon Himself the results of the infringed 'legal liabilities' of those for whom He has rendered satisfaction, they were penal" (*In Understanding*, 159). H. E. Guillebaud uses the term "vicarious punishment" but with a *caveat* against its misuse (*Why the Cross?*, 144–145); this formulation goes back at least to J. H. Heidegger, cited in Heppe, *Reformed Dogmatics*, 468.

Bearing shame and scoffing rude,
In my place condemned he stood;
Sealed my pardon with his blood:
Alleluia, what a Saviour! (P. P. Bliss).

Salvation is available to sinful human beings through the death of Christ, in which he bears the consequences of sin. These consequences constitute the penalty due to sin, rightly called a penalty because it is painful and deprives the sinner of life with God and all its blessings. In this way, the holy and loving God upholds righteousness through judging sinners and saving those who accept what he has done in his Son on their behalf and instead of them.

Nevertheless, this does not free us from the obligation to ask how we can present this doctrine in ways that do not lead to misrepresentation and misunderstanding. As I indicated, I have not entered into this area. It must suffice to have presented a case that, I believe, helps to vindicate the traditional evangelical understanding of the atonement as an expression of the central motif in the New Testament, and I hope that it has provided an understanding of it that can command general assent.

3 "Raised for Our Justification"

It is a remarkable fact that there are many monographs on the theology of the death of Christ, but very few, by comparison, on the theology of his resurrection.[1] Within the latter group of writings, attention has mostly been devoted to the historicity of the resurrection of Christ, and to its significance in relation to the future resurrection of believers. Interest also centers on the role of the resurrection in relation to the present new life of believers. But how is it a saving event? Indeed, is it a saving event? Our goal is to understand Romans 4:25 which declares that Jesus our Lord "was delivered over to death for our sins and was raised to life for our justification." Here justification, which we would probably closely associate with the death of Christ, is specifically tied to his resurrection. How can this be so? We shall approach the text indirectly by considering the wider New Testament context of teaching about the resurrection.

The place of the resurrection in the gospel

At the outset, we need to recognize that two aspects of what happened to Christ after his death need to be distinguished carefully for the sake of theological analysis. One is the

---

[1] Künneth, W. *The Theology of the Resurrection*. London: SCM Press, 1965; Gaffin, R. B. *The Centrality of the Resurrection: A Study in Paul's Soteriology*. Grand Rapids, MI: Baker, 1978; Harris, M. J. *Raised Immortal: The relation between resurrection and immortality in New Testament teaching*. London: Marshall, Morgan and Scott, 1983; Stanley, D. M. *Christ's Resurrection in Pauline Soteriology*. Rome: Pontifical Biblical Institute, 1961; Wright, N. T. *The Resurrection of the Son of God*. Minneapolis, MN: Fortress, 2003.

resurrection of Christ, namely, his being brought back to life after being put to death, and the other is his ascension and subsequent exaltation to sit at the right hand of God. These two actions are integrally connected as aspects of one event, but there is a danger of some confusion, because either action can be used as a means of referring to the whole event. The resurrection of Christ is not simply a return to the physical life in this world that he had before his crucifixion, but it is his re-entry into the spiritual life that he enjoyed before the incarnation. Likewise, the language of glorification and exaltation can be used to cover the whole event, and, in fact, terms referring specifically to the nature of the event as ascension are sparse outside Acts. Only Luke and Acts narrate the story of the ascension as a separate event from the resurrection. The writer to the Hebrews does not refer to the resurrection in the body of his letter, although clearly he presupposes it when he writes about Jesus entering into heaven (e.g., Heb. 10:24).

The relative functions of the death and resurrection of Jesus in relation to salvation are variously expressed in the New Testament.

First, in the writings of Paul, on which I focus because they provide the immediate literary context for Romans 4:25, we can observe how there are passages where the dying and rising of Jesus are closely linked together as one saving event (Rom. 8:34; 14:9; 1 Cor. 15:3–5; 2 Cor. 5:15; 1 Thess. 4:14).[2]

The fullest text of this kind is 1 Corinthians 15:3–5: the summary of the gospel as it was handed down to Paul and preached by him. According to this text, "Christ died for our sins according to the Scriptures." This is then followed by a reference to his burial and resurrection. It is universally agreed that here Paul cites a succinct account of the gospel that was shared with other Christians. It was not his own idiosyncratic version of it. At first sight, the reference to death for our sins is not absolutely essential to the point that he is

---

[2] Wilckens, U. *Der Brief an die Römer.* Zürich: Benziger/Neukirchen: Neukirchener, 1978, I, 280, draws attention to the similar passages in Ignatius, Rom. 6:1; Polycarp, Phil. 9:2.

making, which is primarily a defense of the resurrection. This demonstrates how fundamental the salvific nature of Jesus' death is for Paul. Paul's point, however, is the crucial one that the death, by itself, is not sufficient to deal with sins; he goes on to say: "if Christ has not been raised, your faith is futile; you are still in your sins" (1 Cor. 15:17). From what follows, it is clear that human beings are delivered from the death that Paul regards as the wages of sin through being raised to a new life, in the same way as Christ was raised (1 Cor. 15:21–22). Moreover, this resurrection of believers is not simply like Christ's resurrection, but it comes about through their being united with Christ. Here, then, it is made absolutely clear that the death of Christ would have no saving efficacy apart from his resurrection.

A second type of material is where the death of Jesus is described as the basis for salvation without any reference to the resurrection. Typical examples of such passages are Romans 3:21–26; 2 Corinthians 5:18–21; Ephesians 1:7; Colossians 1:19–20. Yet even these passages stand in broader contexts where the resurrection is also mentioned.

In a third type of material, it was possible for early Christians to sum up the gospel without mention of the atoning significance of the death of Christ, but with some reference to his resurrection or exaltation. Four examples of this can be given.

The first example is the important teaching in Romans 10:5–13 about how people are justified and saved. This passage is all the more significant precisely because it stands in the context of the failure of the Jews to achieve righteousness by the works of the law (Rom. 10:1–5). It also occurs after the long account in chapter 3 about how justification comes to believers through the sacrificial death of Christ. Yet, when Paul reaches the climax of his statement, he declares that what is required for people to be saved is that they declare verbally that "Jesus is Lord" and believe inwardly that God raised him from the dead. He goes on to say: "It is with your heart that you believe and are justified, and it is with your mouth that you profess your faith and are saved." Further, he adds the scriptural support of Joel 2:32

that "everyone who calls on the name of the Lord will be saved" (Rom. 10:13).

Being justified and being saved are here two different ways of describing the same event, and, consequently, Paul means pretty much: "If you believe in your heart and confess with your mouth that Jesus was raised from the dead and is Lord, you will be justified and saved." We might have expected Paul to say: "If you believe that Christ died for your sins, you will be saved," but he doesn't. He is concerned here with the problem of Jews who thought that they could be saved apart from faith in Christ, and, therefore, his argument is shaped to deal with this point. His argument begins with the fact that the prophet Joel says that it is if you call on the Lord that you will be saved; Paul takes this to mean that you cannot be saved except by calling on the Lord (rather than by trying to establish your own righteousness). But then he makes the point that the Christ whom God raised from the dead is the Lord, and, therefore, even though in the time of Joel, people called on Yahweh for salvation, now they must call on the Lord Jesus Christ. It is the *identity* of the Lord which is the crucial issue here. Consequently, the lack of emphasis on the atoning death of Jesus may not be too surprising.

A second relevant passage is 1 Thessalonians 1:9–10. In his account of the conversion of the Gentile readers that Paul describes here, he relates how they turned from their idols to God, the one and only God of the Jews, to serve him and to wait for the coming of his Son from heaven, namely Jesus, whom he raised from the dead and who will deliver them from the future wrath at the day of judgement. Here salvation (or deliverance) is linked to Jesus, but it is not explained how he is able to deliver people from wrath. The reference to his being raised from the dead explains how it is that he is in heaven, with the implied assumption that a person who has been raised from the dead is able to return from heaven. Elsewhere, in the same letter, it is made clear that future salvation is received through our Lord Jesus Christ who died for us (1 Thess. 5:9–10). But, although the connection of salvation to the death of Jesus is made there, the gospel can be summarized without reference to it.

A third important passage is Philippians 2:6-11, where the life and death of Jesus are used to form the basis for an appeal to believers to show the same obedience and humility as he did. However, the death is not explained as a saving event. Many consider this to be a pre-Pauline composition incorporated by Paul in his letter. I, however, think there are good grounds for ascribing it to Paul himself.[3] It is arguable that, once we recognize that this passage was probably composed by Paul for its present exemplary purpose, the lack of reference to the saving significance of the death is not especially remarkable. Nevertheless, the text is noteworthy in that Paul did not think it necessary to say anything here about the purpose of Christ's death.[4]

And, finally, in this catalogue, there is a set of passages from the evangelism in Acts, where, in the gospel messages preached to unbelievers, the death of Jesus is never said to be a death for us or for our sins. Rather, the death is seen as the obstacle to accepting that Jesus is the Messiah; not only was he not accepted as such by the Jewish leaders and many Jewish people, but also he was actually put to death by them. The preachers overcome this obstacle by pointing to the important fact that God raised Jesus from the dead, thereby undoing the evil act, and, at the same time, exalting him to his right hand so that Jesus could function as Lord and Messiah. How Jesus' death is related to this as a saving event is not explained in the evangelistic sermons.

We thus see several ways of presenting the significance of Jesus' death and resurrection. First, both may be mentioned together in a way that shows they were seen as a unity, not surprisingly in view of the temporal proximity of the one to

---

[3] For the former view, see Martin, R. P. *Carmen Christi: Philippians ii.5–11 in recent interpretation and in the setting of early Christian worship.* Grand Rapids, MI: Eerdmans, 1983²; originally Cambridge: Cambridge University Press, 1967. For the latter view, see Fee, G. D. *Paul's Letter to the Philippians.* Grand Rapids, MI: Eerdmans, 1995, 43–46.

[4] Contrast 1 Peter 2:21–25, where Peter, having begun to give his readers a portrayal of Christ as an example to them in his suffering, just cannot stop himself from going on to express powerfully the saving consequences of those sufferings.

the other, and the fact that the resurrection presupposes the death. Second, there may be an exclusive emphasis on the death and its effects in such a way that it might seem that the resurrection has nothing to add to it. Third, there may be mention of the resurrection with little or no reference to the death and its significance.

Although Romans 4:25 belongs formally to the first category of passages, where both the death and resurrection are mentioned, it stands close to this third category of passages in that here there is specific emphasis on the place of the resurrection in the saving event.[5] While recognizing that Christ was delivered up to death because of our sins (or to do something about them), it relates justification not so much to his death as to his being raised. Here we should also mention Romans 5:10 which appears to make a distinction between reconciliation through the death of Christ and future salvation through his life; here the reference is generally understood to be to his resurrection life.[6]

How, then, are we to understand the place of the resurrection in these specific references to justification and final salvation? And how does Paul's teaching relate to that elsewhere in the New Testament?

We can distinguish this theme from some other related ones.[7] For example, one important aspect of the significance of the resurrection of Jesus as a saving event is the way in which it functions as the guarantee and pattern for the resurrection of believers (1 Cor. 15). However, consideration of this topic would divert us from our concern with comparatively neglected problems of the relationship of Christ's resurrection to sin and death and the justification of sinners.

---

[5] In its context, this emphasis is undoubtedly related to the preceding verses in which Abraham is presented as believing in the God who raises the dead.

[6] E.g., Moo, D. *The Epistle to the Romans.* Grand Rapids, MI: Eerdmans, 1996, 312.

[7] Questions such as the historicity of the resurrection of Christ and the nature of his resurrection body lie outside our interest here. Needless to say, the resurrection would have no saving effects if it had not happened.

The relationship between the death and resurrection of Jesus

Divine approval of the crucified Christ

Perhaps the most common, popular explanation for the connection between the death and resurrection of Jesus is to argue that the resurrection is God's confirmation and acceptance of what Christ did in his death, giving his sacrifice "the stamp of God's approval."[8] There is general recognition that the resurrection is the act of the Father in raising the dead Christ, and not the self-raising of Christ. Christ does not raise himself, even though he may be said to have the power to do so (John 10:18).[9] Consequently, as the act of the Father, the resurrection can be understood as his affirmation of the Son openly to the people.

This type of divine action can be seen on a broader scale in Acts 10:38–39, where we are told that Jesus was enabled to do his mighty acts because God was with him, and in Acts 2:22, where Jesus is "a man accredited by God to you by miracles, wonders and signs which God did among you through him." Similarly, Hebrews 2:4 says that the apostles' preaching is accompanied by God's testimony "by signs, wonders and various miracles, and by gifts of the Holy Spirit distributed according to his will." Although this testimony primarily confirms the message, in fact it demonstrates that salvation comes through Jesus and what he did.

Although the resurrection is not specifically mentioned in these passages, it does figure in this way in the conclusion of the Areopagus address, where Paul explains that the proof that Jesus will be the future judge of the world is the fact that God has raised him from the dead (Acts 17:31).

---

[8] Sanday, W., and A. C. Headlam. *A Critical and Exegetical Commentary on the Epistle to the Romans.* Edinburgh: T & T Clark, 1902[5], 117. So recently (for example), Schreiner, T. R. *Romans.* Grand Rapids, MI: Baker, 1998, 244.

[9] Marshall, I. H. "The Resurrection in the Acts of the Apostles." In *Apostolic History and the Gospel: Biblical and Historical Essays Presented to F. F. Bruce,* edited by W. W. Gasque and R. P. Martin. Exeter: Paternoster Press, 1970, 101–103.

The resurrection, therefore, although witnessed by only a few people, is proclaimed as God's supreme affirmation of Jesus to all people. Consequently, an important part of early Christian apologetic is the way in which the apostles' preaching that Jesus is Messiah and Lord is backed up by their witness to the resurrection of Jesus; they have seen and heard the risen Lord.[10]

But the resurrection is more than simply a confirmation of the status and identity of Jesus to a human audience. It is also God's action, which undoes what evil human beings and the devil sought to accomplish by putting Jesus to death. They thought that, by putting him to death, they could bring his work to an end and discredit his message. The resurrection is the event in which God undoes what they have done through overcoming death and its effects.

God did so because death could not hold Jesus (Acts 2:24). This means that there was something about Jesus that prevented his death from being permanent. What was it? It was probably the fact that Jesus believed in the God who delivers those who call to him from death and decay. This is in accordance with the David's firm statement in Scripture that he will not be abandoned to death because God will deliver him (Acts 2:25–28, citing Ps. 16:8–11). This is a more likely explanation than one which draws conclusions from the divine nature of Jesus as the Son of God.[11] Thus, implicitly rather than explicitly, in Acts, the raising of the Messiah is God's affirmation of him as the Messiah, despite human and satanic opposition.

However, this line of argument does not specifically relate the resurrection of Jesus to the achieving of salvation on behalf of sinful humanity. In Acts, it is not directly said that

---

[10] Although the fact of the empty tomb does not figure in the preaching in Acts, the stories in the Gospels were presumably employed for this purpose.

[11] In an earlier discussion, I said that it was because Jesus was the Messiah and the Messiah could not be held by death. This could be taken to mean that God could not allow death to conquer his agent. It might also be the case that the Messiah has faith in God to which God is bound to respond. Cf. Marshall, I. H. *The Acts of the Apostles.* Leicester: IVP, 1980, 76.

Christ dies for sinners[12] and that God accepts this action. The resurrection is not seen as God's approval of what Christ has done for sinners. Rather, the resurrection is how God undoes the acts of the wicked people who put Jesus to death, and how he affirms that Jesus is the Messiah and Lord, and thus the author of salvation. This may not be all that Luke-Acts has to say on the matter, as we shall note later, but the interpretation of the resurrection simply as the undoing of the slaying of Jesus does not integrally relate it to the achieving of salvation.

The heavenly offering made by Christ

More promising for our investigation is the path taken in Hebrews. Here the saving action by the Son is seen as having two parts, like the making and offering of a sacrifice. The first stage is the slaying of the sacrificial victim; the second is the offering of the blood to God or the burning of the carcass so that the smoke ascends to God. A gift or offering to God is thus symbolized by these actions (Heb. 9:7). The death of Jesus, as the victim, is followed by the entry of Jesus, as high priest, bearing the blood of his own sacrifice to God. The writer conceives the heaven into which Jesus enters as being like a temple (or rather it is the antitype of earthly temples)[13] where God is really present, and there Jesus presents his sacrifice to God, on the basis of which forgiveness is available to sinners.

The accent thus falls on the action of the risen Son and High Priest. Two surprising points stand out. First, Hebrews does not use the term "raise" (except in Heb. 13:20, a benediction whose language may well rest on tradition rather than being a reflection of the author's distinctive theology). Rather, Jesus passes through the heavens (Heb. 4:14; 9:11), enters heaven

---

[12] The thought is, of course, explicit in Luke 22:19–20 and implicit in Acts 20:28.

[13] We might be tempted to say that the author pictures heaven on the analogy of the earthly tabernacle, but the writer manifestly thought that the earthly tabernacle was built on the model of the heavenly tabernacle, just as described by God to Moses in Exodus.

on our behalf (Heb. 6:20; 9:12, 24, 25), and sits down when his task is done (Heb. 8:1; 10:12; 12:2). God's action in raising Jesus thus retreats to the background, and the writer simply assumes that, having died, Jesus somehow could have access to heaven.[14] There is no action of God the Father, and, indeed, no mention of resurrection as the mode of entry to heaven.[15] Thus the heavenly entry of Jesus is understood in Hebrews more as his own action. This contrasts with the way, depicted elsewhere in the New Testament, in which God raises him, glorifies him and honors him. In Hebrews, Christ continues to be the agent of salvation in his heavenly activity. Perhaps we should understand this in the light of God's appointment of Jesus as high priest (Heb. 5:5-6), which presumably preceded his entry to heaven; having obtained this delegated authority from God, he was able to act on the basis of it.

So the resurrection as such has moved out of the picture. The accent has shifted from the raising of Jesus to his entry into heaven to appear for us in God's presence. But there is something else surprising that takes place. All that we are told is that Christ appears on behalf of sinners, makes his offering to God, sits down and continues to intercede, but nothing is said about God's acceptance of the offering. No doubt the acceptance can be assumed, since the throne that we approach is a throne of grace (Heb. 4:16), but it is not part of the story. What Christ has done is accepted by God, but the divine acceptance is not described: is this because the Old Testament pattern does not contain anything comparable?

A further point should be noted. Hebrews clearly distinguishes two aspects to what Christ does in heaven. The one is the making of the offering to God, and this is stated emphatically to be "once for all" (Heb. 7:27; 9:12, 26, 28; 10:10; cf. 10:14). The sacrifice has been made and offered; then Christ sits down. There is nothing that needs to be

---

[14] To be sure, there is reference to the crowning of Jesus (Heb. 2:5–9) which implies a divine recognition of Jesus. Also Jesus' reign at the right hand of God rests on God's invitation (Heb. 1:13).

[15] Here the possible contrast between resurrection and heavenly access is most clearly present.

repeated.[16] The other is that, from his sitting position at the right hand of God, he makes intercession for sinners (Heb. 7:25). Thus his role as high priest continues, but it is a role of intercession based on the sacrifice once for all made and offered.

It may be noted in passing that Protestant, evangelical Christians have rightly insisted that the way in which Hebrews expresses things takes away the need for any further sacrifice or any re-enactment of the one sacrifice, specifically, in the Roman Catholic understanding, that the mass is in some way a re-presentation of what Christ has done, whereby the bread and wine become the actual body and blood of Christ, which are then offered by a functionary who is called a priest. Hence popular language refers to "the sacrifice of the mass."[17]

Consequently, Protestants generally have denied any particularly sacrificial role to the minister at the Lord's Supper,[18] although there are tendencies in many rituals to regard the bread and wine as offerings by the people to God which he then takes and uses to be vehicles of salvation to them. This concept of God using what we offer and transforming it is entirely against the spirit of the New Testament in which God is the giver and we are the recipients of sheer grace.[19]

---

[16] Stibbs, A. M. *The Finished Work of Christ.* London: Tyndale Press, 1954.

[17] Hildebrandt, F. *I offered Christ: A Protestant Study of the Mass.* London: Epworth, 1967, has noted how the phrase "to offer Christ," used to describe the action of the priest in the mass, was used in a different sense by John Wesley to refer to the offering of salvation to sinners by the preacher.

[18] An exception is Collins, C. J. "The Eucharist as Christian Sacrifice: How Patristic Authors Can Help Us Read the Bible." *WTJ* 66 (2004): 1–23, who argues that the Lord's Supper reflects the Old Testament peace-offering and that the ministry of those who lead it constitutes a special priesthood, different from that of the laity.

[19] See, for example, *The Methodist Worship Book.* Peterborough: Methodist Publishing House, 1999, where the bread and wine are brought to the table along with the offerings of the people; they are ambiguously referred to in prayer as "these gifts of bread and wine," but whether they are God's gifts or the gifts of the people that God takes and uses is not entirely clear; certainly the prayer on p. 136 suggests the latter, but the prayer on p. 168 clearly indicates the former.

There is, nevertheless, an ongoing role of intercession. The Son is presented as being himself active on behalf of sinners, and the picture is intended to denote the ongoing efficacy of his sacrifice. It avails "for all time," "to the uttermost." The basic point that emerges from all this is that Christ's work in atonement is not completed until something has been done in heaven that ratifies what has been done on the cross; at that point, the sacrifice is complete and Christ has no need to "enter heaven to offer himself again and again" as the Jewish high priest did on his annual visit (Heb. 9:25-28). The act of sacrifice and the offering of the sacrifice are theoretically distinguishable, and each must take place. They form a unity, and neither is effective without the other. Here we have possibly some kind of parallel and guide that may help us to understand Paul's somewhat different presentation.

Victory over the power of evil

The resurrection has an important place in the Christus Victor type of understanding of the work of Christ. Here the central thought is that death is, as it were, administered by the devil who is paying his servants the wages of sin (Heb. 2:14; Rom. 6:23). The devil seeks to overcome Christ, and the latter succumbs to death. Apparently evil has won the victory. But Jesus' resurrection shows that death could not overcome him, and he shares this victory with believers. On this view of things, one might expect that it would be Christ himself who conquers death, but, as we have seen, the thought is more that God raises him from the dead. Thus Father and Son are closely united here as the agents of victory and the ensuing salvation.

Yet, in Hebrews 2:14, it is through death that Jesus destroys the one who has the power of death, and sets free his captives. However, we need to be careful how this is understood. It is, apparently, Jesus' death that constitutes the victory over the devil here, and there is no reference to his resurrection. Can it be that the victory over death lies in the fact that Christ died one death on behalf of all, with the result that the devil can no longer have any power over believers because they have in effect already died in Christ's death? And is the victory of Jesus to be seen further in his gracious willingness to submit to death, as compared with the attitude of human beings for whom it is the due punishment for their sins?[20] In any case, must we not say that no early Christian could have understood the death of Jesus as victory over the devil without closely linking the resurrection to it?

Understanding Romans 4:25

After this survey of other material on the significance of the resurrection, we now come at last to a consideration of Romans 4:25. This verse makes two statements in parallel. Whatever else they convey, these statements emphasize that both Christ's death and his resurrection were for our benefit.[21]

First, we are told that Jesus was delivered over [to death] because of our transgressions. The verb "deliver" is used in three ways elsewhere with reference to the death of Jesus. It can refer to the action of Judas in handing over Jesus to the authorities who crucified him (Mark 3:19; 14:21; cf. 1 Cor. 11:23). But it is also used for the action of God who handed over his Son to death (Rom. 8:32) or reflexively of the action of Jesus in surrendering himself to death (Gal. 2:20; Eph. 5:2, 25). In view of the proximity of Romans 4:25a to Romans 8:32, and the parallelism with Romans 4:25b, a reference to the action of God the Father is most probable here. Behind the phrase probably lie such statements as Isaiah 53:12 LXX (his soul was handed over to death) and Isaiah 53:6 (the

---

[20] Another "Christus Victor" text is Colossians 2:15. Here Christ either divested himself of the powers or disarmed them and, in so doing, made a public spectacle of them, i.e., made their defeat clear to all, and he did so "in it" or "in him." The subject of the verb (whether God or Christ) is not clear, and the prepositional phrase could refer to Christ or the cross. Here again the decisive element is the cross, i.e., the death of Christ, rather than the resurrection.

[21] See Lowe, B. A. "Oh διά! How is Romans 4:25 to be understood?" *JTS* ns 57 (2006): 149–57; Lowe finds an echo of the use of the first person plural in Isaiah 53:4–6.

Lord handed him over to our sins). The statement that it was because of our sins that he was handed over to death agrees with the repeated statements elsewhere in the New Testament that he died "for" our sins.[22] If it had not been for our sins, he would not have died, and hence there is some connection between our sins and his death. The conjunction "because of" (*dia*) here is most commonly understood as retrospective and causal, although some scholars take it as prospective and interpret it to mean "with a view to doing something about our sins."[23] In any case, this latter sense is surely implied.

---

[22] The two prepositions used are *huper* (1 Cor. 15:3; Gal. 1:4; cf. Heb. 10:12) and *peri* (Rom. 8:3; 1 Pet. 3:18; 1 John 2:2; 4:10; see also Heb. 10:6, 8, 18, 26; 13:11 where *peri* is used of Old Testament sacrifices).

[23] The sense of *dia* in the two parts of the verse is disputed.

1. Some take the two prepositional phrases in the same retrospective, broadly causal, way: "He died because we sinned and rose because we were justified"; cf. Morris, L. *The Apostolic Preaching of the Cross*. London: Tyndale Press, 1965[3], 288–289.

2. Some take the two prepositional phrases in the same prospective way: He died "in order to atone for [our trespasses]" and "to bring about [our justification]"; cf. Lohse, E. *Der Brief an die Römer*. Göttingen: Vandenhoeck und Ruprecht, 2003, 162 n. 19, who says that both must be taken in the same way as "final" (presumably with a view to dealing with our sins and our justification).

3. Many take the first phrase retrospectively and the second prospectively: "He died because we sinned and rose with a view to our justification"; e.g., Cranfield, C. E. B. *A Critical and Exegetical Commentary on the Epistle to the Romans*. Edinburgh: T & T Clark, 1975, I, 251–252; Dunn, J. D. G. *Romans 1–8*. Dallas, TX: Word, 1988, 224–225.

It has been suggested that Paul is using the device of parallelism rhetorically to say essentially the same thing in two different ways, so that the meaning is determined by combining what is said in the two clauses. Hence the rendering: "Jesus died and rose again because of our trespasses and justification"'; Taylor, V. *The Atonement in New Testament Teaching*. London: Epworth, 1945[2], 67. Presumably, on this understanding, the two occurrences of the preposition are taken to have the same force, whether retrospective or prospective. While this is a true statement (since justification is clearly related to the cross in Rom. 3:24–25), it does not do justice to Paul's careful formulation in this verse; cf. Hooker, M. D. "Raised for our acquittal (Rom. 4,25)," in *Resurrection in the New Testament: Festschrift J. Lambrecht*, edited by R Bieringer et al. Leuven: Leuven University Press, 2002, 323–341 (323).

Second, in parallel, we are told that Jesus was raised because of our justification.[24] In the previous verse, Paul states that God will credit righteousness to those who believe in him as the God who raised Jesus our Lord from death. This anticipates and coheres with the statement in Romans 10:9, where justification and salvation are for those who believe that God raised Jesus from the dead. Paul can thus speak of both believing that God raised Jesus from the dead and believing in the God who raised Jesus. Belief that God did something, and believing in the God who did it are two complementary aspects of the single action of faith. In this action of faith, we believe that something is true about what God is and does and put our confident trust in him to act accordingly. The verb "to believe" here is linked to its object by the preposition "on" (*epi*) and suggests the idea of confidently resting upon this God and what he has done.[25] So confidence is placed on God in his capacity to raise the dead.

The issue is partly the power of God to do the impossible, as is to be seen in the comparison with the action of Abraham in believing that God could give him and Sarah a child despite apparently impossible circumstances. That the impossibility of resurrection was an issue in the first century, as also in the twenty-first, is clearly apparent from 1 Corinthians 15; Acts 17:32; 26:8. But there is more to it than simply the power of God. God does something impossible in order to achieve a promised goal. In the case of Abraham, the miracle of Isaac's birth took place so that Abraham might become a father of many nations. Consequently, in the case of Christian believers, the raising of Jesus must play some part in the act of justification.

But what is the connection? Here we run into an ambiguity. If we take the prepositional phrase "because of" in the first clause in v. 25 in a retrospective sense, and then interpret the second clause in parallel with it, this would give a statement

---

[24] *Dikaiōsis* is the process of justification; cf. Romans 5:18.
[25] Cf. Romans 4:5; 9:33; 1 Timothy 1:16; 1 Peter 2:6; Acts 9:42; 16:31; 22:19.

in which God raised Christ "because our justification had taken place." In that case, the resurrection was not part of the action that led to justification, but rather something that followed it and simply confirms it. Alternatively, if we take the first clause prospectively to mean that Christ was delivered over to death in order to atone for our trespasses, then we can also take the second clause prospectively: Christ was raised from the dead in order to bring about our justification.

However, whether or not we take the first clause retrospectively, the second clause by itself can certainly have this prospective sense, namely that Christ was raised from the dead with a view to our justification, i.e., so that we might be justified. This is a standard use of the preposition *dia*.[26] With the majority of scholars, I shall assume that this is the correct interpretation.[27]

So we have a statement in which justification is tied in some way to Jesus' resurrection. This is an interesting shift from Romans 3 where everything rests on Jesus' death and nothing is said about his resurrection. However, we shall find hints elsewhere that salvation depends on something more than just the death of Jesus.

But in what sense had Christ to be raised so that we might be justified? It is remarkable that some leading commentators barely discuss the issue at all.[28]

---

[26] Some defenders of the retrospective sense in the first clause argue that the preposition must have the same sense in the second clause. To this objection that it is unlikely that Paul could use the same preposition in two different ways in the same sentence we can reply that in fact he does so elsewhere, and the difference in usage is quite possible despite the parallelism. There are possible cases in Romans 8:10; 11:28; compare the varied uses of *en* in 1 Timothy 3:16. Since "sins" and "justification" are terms of two different kinds, a shift in the force of the prepositions governing them is not surprising, perhaps even necessary.

[27] See Bird, M. F. "Justified by Christ's Resurrection: A Neglected aspect of Paul's Doctrine of Justification." *SBET* 22 (2004): 72–91, here 83–84 (see now *The Saving Righteousness of God*. Milton Keynes, Paternoster, 2007, 40–59). I am indebted to Dr. Bird for his helpful comments during the composition of this paper.

[28] E.g., Cranfield, 251–52. Dunn, 225 and 240–241 (he notes justifying grace has to be accompanied by life-giving power); Moo, 288–290 (one sentence!);

One possibility, which can be maintained as part of a total interpretation, is that the resurrection is the event through which the new era of salvation comes into existence, so that those who belong to Christ can share in it.[29]

One suggested function of the resurrection here is to raise Jesus to the right hand of God to intercede for us (Rom. 8:34).[30] However, the reference in Romans 4:25 is to resurrection and not, specifically, to exaltation to God's right hand nor to intercession. This interpretation requires that we read a lot into the verse.

Another possibility is that the resurrection places Jesus in the position where he is able to offer and declare forgiveness to sinners, just as, in Acts, Peter says that God raises and exalts Jesus so that he might have this function (Acts 5:31). However, in Paul's usage, it is normally God the Father who offers justification rather than Christ.

More promising is the proposal, already mentioned, that the resurrection offers the essential evidence that God accepted Jesus' atoning sacrifice on the basis of which justification becomes available. However, put in this form, the proposal remains vague and needs closer attention.[31]

One possibility is that the resurrection is simply God's vindication of the death of Jesus, and signifies that it has been effective in making justification possible.[32] The resurrection

---

Osborne, G. R. *Romans.* Downers Grove: IVP, 2004, 122–23; Witherington III, B. with D. Hyatt. *Paul's Letter to the Romans: A Socio-Rhetorical Commentary.* Grand Rapids, MI: Eerdmans, 2004, 129.

[29] Wilckens, *Brief*, I, 278–79, comes within range of this interpretation of Romans 4:25 by seeing the breaking in of the new eon in the resurrection of Jesus; believers share in this through belonging to Christ.

[30] Cf. Haacker, K. *Der Brief des Paulus an die Römer.* Leipzig: Evangelische Verlagsanstalt, 1999, 111, n. 14.

[31] Here I am particularly indebted to the recent work of M. F. Bird who helpfully brings together and summarizes various suggestions that have been offered before developing one in particular.

[32] Harris, *Raised Immortal*, 164–165; Stott, J. *The Cross of Christ.* Leicester: IVP, 1986, 238–239; Stott is fearful lest anything should detract from the completeness of Christ's sin-bearing on the cross: "The resurrection did not achieve our deliverance from sin and death, but has brought us an assurance of both." Cf. Ridderbos, H. *Paul: An Outline of his Theology.*

is then a demonstration to human beings that God has accepted what Christ has done.[33] Certainly, this ties in with the apologetic function of the resurrection that we have seen elsewhere, especially in Acts. And it would provide visible evidence of an unseen event. But it seems to confuse the achievement of justification with the corroboration of justification, and it rests on what we have seen to be the less likely understanding of the syntax of the phrase.[34] Above all, it is very odd to make confession of belief in the raising of Jesus the ground of salvation, if his resurrection is merely the guarantee that his death for us was effective. Rather, we would have expected that what was necessary, as the actual divine basis for our salvation, was belief in the fact that Jesus died for our sins.

The other way of taking the statement is to see the vindication as an essential part of the process in which Christ bears the consequences of human sin. God accepts that Christ has borne the penalty of human sin and does so by raising him from the death that he suffered on behalf of humanity. This point is put most effectively by W. Künneth:

> The resurrection can be the realizing of salvation because it not only enables us to see the death of Jesus as punishment imposed by God, but in awakening Jesus from death remits this punishment, and so liberates from guilt... In the Risen One the new curse-free relationship between God and man is given. In him the new reality of being objectively reconciled with God has taken concrete form... *God justifies the sinner because of the new situation of being reconciled and justified which is created by the raising of the Crucified. In this situation sinful man, in so far as he participates in it through Christ, is qualified as just before God.*[35]

London: SPCK, 1977, 167; see also Jewett, R. *Romans*. Minneapolis, MN: Fortress Press, 2007, 343.

[33] E.g., "his resurrection... is the apologetic basis of salvation" (Osborne, *Romans*, 123).

[34] It would be a possible interpretation if the prepositional phrase was retrospective, "raised because our justification has taken place," i.e., as evidence that it has happened.

[35] Künneth, *Theology*, 157–158.

On this view, the resurrection is God's release of Christ from the punishment of sin that he is bearing; he remits any continuation of the punishment. Hence there is now the possibility of a new relationship between God and the man whom he has judged in death, and so God can now forgive sinners. This goes beyond the interpretation that sees the resurrection as God's recognition that Christ has paid the penalty for sin; it makes explicit God's granting of the decisive remission of the guilt that Christ has been bearing, and makes him the representative Man in whom we can be justified.

Somewhat similar statements are made by other writers.[36] They express in various ways the view that "The resurrection is Christ's justification in which believers participate by faith."[37] It is "a constitutive, transforming action… It is Christ's justification."[38] "God 'justified' Jesus by raising him from the dead: the one verdict has already been given (following the act of obedience on the cross); by faith Christians enter into Christ and are associated with that verdict."[39] "Jesus' resurrection was the divine *vindication* of him as Messiah, 'son

---

[36] Stanley, *Christ's Resurrection*, 275, holds that Christ becomes the second Adam through his resurrection, but he does not link this to Christ's bearing of the consequences of sin. Cf. Bird, "Justified," 76–77.

[37] Bird, "Justified," 79.

[38] Gaffin, *Centrality*, 122–124. His point is well-summarized in the statement in a later article: "As our substitute, a crucified but unresurrected Christ still bears the guilt of our sins; as long as he remains in a state of death, its penal force continues and he (and believers) are unjustified. The resurrection is his de facto justification and so secures the believer's justification. This is the likely sense in Romans 4:25" (Gaffin, R. B. "Atonement in the Pauline Corpus: 'The Scandal of the Cross.'" In C. E. Hill and F. A. James III. *The Glory of the Atonement: Biblical, Historical and Practical Perspectives*. Downers Grove: IVP, 2004, 160. Gaffin refers to earlier recognition of the point; cf. Heppe, H. *Reformed Dogmatics*. London: George Allen and Unwin, 1950, 498–499, citing Olevian: "Just as by giving the Son to death the Father actually condemned all our sins in him, the Father also by raising Christ up from the dead, acquitted Christ of our sin-guilt and us in Christ."

[39] Head, P. M. "Jesus' Resurrection in Pauline Thought: A Study in Romans." In *Proclaiming the Resurrection: Papers from the First Oak Hill Annual School of Theology*, edited by P. M. Head. Carlisle: Paternoster Press, 1998, 69 (58–80).

of God' in that sense, the representative of Israel and thence of the world... God's raising of Jesus from the dead was therefore the act in which justification – the vindication of all God's people 'in Christ' – was contained in a nutshell."[40]

A particularly influential contribution is that of M. D. Hooker who states that Christ "was raised in order that we might share his acquittal (pronounced at his resurrection)."[41] The argument in Romans 5:12–19 "suggests that the acquittal of the many depends on the acquittal of Christ. This acquittal, which leads to life for the many, would have taken place at the resurrection, an act of vindication which established his righteousness."[42] As Hooker has demonstrated, the *dikaiōma* in Romans 5:18 should have the same sense as in v. 16, and refer to the vindication or acquittal of Christ by God that then results in the *dikaiōsis* or justification of all who are united with him through faith.

Other texts can be drawn into the discussion. Thus we are now in a position to appreciate the brief allusion to Christ's life in Romans 5:10. The basic thought in the passage is that those who were reconciled to God when they were sinners will *a fortiori* be delivered from the wrath expressed against

---

[40] Wright, *Resurrection*, 248.

[41] Hooker, M. D. *Paul: A Short Introduction.* Oxford: One World, 2003, 94. See especially "Raised for our acquittal."

[42] Hooker, M. D. *From Adam to Christ: Essays on Paul.* Cambridge: CUP, 1990, 29; cf. 39. Other authors move in the same direction. "[Paul] did not regard the effect of the sacrificial death of Christ as complete in itself. The first part required the ratification of the second. The vindication of Christ was also the vindication of those whom he represented" (Dunn, J. D. G. *The Theology of Paul the Apostle.* Grand Rapids, MI: Eerdmans, 1998, 236). "As Christ's death provides the necessary grounds on which God's justifying action can proceed, so his resurrection, by vindicating Christ and freeing him forever from the influence of sin (cf. 6:10), provides for the ongoing power over sins experienced by the believer in union with Christ" (Moo, *Romans*, 290). See also Thrall, M. E. *A Critical and Exegetical Commentary on the Second Epistle to the Corinthians.* Edinburgh: T & T Clark, 1994, 2000, I, 439–444, who argues that, in 2 Corinthians 5:21, Christ is vindicated as righteous through the resurrection and it is this righteous status that is shared with sinners.

sinners at the final judgement.[43] The reconciliation is attributed to the death of God's Son, but the salvation to his life. Here "saved" refers to deliverance at the final judgement, and "life" refers to the resurrection life of Jesus (cf. Rom. 6:10). Thus, in both parts of the statement, final salvation is dependent upon Christ (and not upon ourselves or what we do). Our sins have been dealt with by the death of Christ (with whom we are united); now, as those who are united with him in his life, we are alive to God and, therefore, outside the sphere of wrath. It is thus union with the Christ who died and rose for us that is the basis of our final salvation.[44]

R. B. Gaffin refers to 1 Corinthians 15:17 which states: "If Christ has not been raised, your faith is futile; you are still in your sins." This statement is at least compatible with the view that is being developed: if Christ merely died, the possibility of justification does not exist. For Gaffin, the point is that raising to new life is an essential part of justification, and if Christ has not been raised, justification is not possible. Here we are beginning to see that the traditional understanding of justification may be too inclined to the negative element, namely cancellation of sins, and has not done justice to the positive element, namely creating a new, living relationship with God.[45] Resurrection permeates the theology of Romans.[46]

Somewhat controversial is the interpretation of 1 Timothy 3:16 which Gaffin and Bird share. This states that Christ was not merely vindicated in the Spirit but specifically justified.[47] There is no doubt that the reference in this phrase is to the resurrection/exaltation of Jesus, but commentators differ whether his resurrection/exaltation vindicates the claims

---

[43] Similarly, in the previous verse, justification is attributed to the blood of Christ, but (future) salvation from wrath simply to him.

[44] This encourages the understanding of 2 Corinthians 5:15 as referring to the Christ "who died-and-was-raised for them."

[45] Gaffin, *Centrality*, 123–124; cf. Bird, "Justified," 81.

[46] Bird, "Justified," 81–85.

[47] Gaffin, *Centrality*, 119–122; Bird, "Justified." 85–89; cf. Hooker, *From Adam to Christ*, 34-35.

made by Jesus during his lifetime,[48] or demonstrates the righteousness of the One crucified as an evildoer,[49] or is a stage further after his manifestation in the flesh in which we have "the eschatological confirmation through God, which brings Jesus' function as mediator to completion in regard to the saving will of God."[50] Gaffin wants to see Jesus here as the second Adam who bears death for human guilt and is now confirmed as righteous, i.e., justified.[51] This reads the verse against a broad background of Adamic Christology and Pauline soteriology (seen in 2 Cor. 5:21; Gal. 3;13; 4:5) for which I can find no contextual support.

A background in the LXX of Isaiah 53:11 (with 50:8) is detected by H. Stettler. Where the MT speaks of the Servant justifying many, the LXX describes how God justifies or vindicates the one who serves many: "after the shame which he has endured he is exalted by God and vindicated."[52] But it would probably be going too far to find a reference to a representative justification in the soteriological sense of Christ

---

[48] Mounce, W. D. *Pastoral Epistles.* Nashville, TN: Thomas Nelson, 2000, 227. "Contained in these two lines... is the acknowledgment of the truth of the gospel message, that God came among humankind and introduced a new kind of life" (Towner, P. H. *1–2 Timothy and Titus.* Downers Grove: IVP, 1994, 99).

[49] Roloff, J. *Der erste Brief an Timotheus.* Zürich: Benziger/Neukirchen: Neukirchener, 1988, 205–206. Neudorfer, H.-W. *Der erste Brief des Paulus an Timotheus.* Wuppertal: Brockhaus, 2004, 162, sees it as vindication or justification [same German word] of the one rejected and crucified by men.

[50] Oberlinner, L. *Kommentar zum ersten Timotheusbrief.* Freiburg: Herder, 1994, 166 (my translation).

[51] Gaffin, *Centrality,* 123–124. Similarly, Bird, "Justified," 87–88, who wants to trace a background in Isaiah 53:11, but this verse refers to the Servant vindicating others, not to himself being vindicated/justified.

[52] Stettler, H. *Die Christologie der Pastoralbriefe.* Tübingen: Mohr Siebeck, 1998, 96-98. Isaiah 50:8 refers to God as "he who vindicates me." The presence of allusions to Isaiah 53:5 in Romans 4:25a and to Isaiah 53:9, 11 in Romans 5:16 and 19 was detected by J. Jeremias, *TDNT* V: 706. Bird, "Justified," 87–88, also suggested a background in Isaiah 53:11 for the motif in both Romans 4:25 and 1 Timothy 3:16; his case is strengthened by Stettler's observation that the LXX gives better support to this proposal than does the MT.

here. It is doubtful, then, whether the justification of Christ in this narrow soteriological sense can be said to be taught by this verse, but it certainly refers to God's confirmation of him in broad terms. It is on the basis of this that the missionary preaching and its results in the later part of the verse can take place.

The most that can be said, then, is that these three passages may contain thinking along the same lines as Romans 4:25, and do not constitute an obstacle to our interpretation of it.

It seems to me that here we have a decisive step forward in understanding the relation of the resurrection to justification. It goes beyond the simple understanding of Christ's resurrection in terms of God's vindication of him, purely as a demonstration to humanity that he was the Messiah after all and that his sacrifice has been effective. Rather, in raising Christ from death after he has taken upon himself the sins of the world and died, God is not so much vindicating what Christ has done and saying that he approves of it, but is bringing him back from the dead as the One who is now just and experiencing the new life that God grants to those whose sin has been taken away; this is happening representatively to Christ so that believers may share in this new life. In the cross God's condemnation of sin is demonstrated and carried out, Christ bears the sin and so God declares that sin has been taken away; and Christ is representatively justified so that those who believe and are united with him share in this justification. Hence, the resurrection is essential to the saving act in that it is not merely God saying that Christ has done what is necessary; rather, God himself has to carry out the act of pardon on the basis of what Christ has done, and he does so. Thus Christ was raised for our justification, and, without this raising of Christ, we would not be justified.

According to Bird, the death and resurrection have different functions but work in tandem to achieve justification: "In the resurrection God's declaration of vindication and the enactment of it are manifested in the resurrection of Christ."[53] The resurrection is to be seen as the justification of Christ

---

[53] Bird, "Justified," 84.

as the last Adam, and, consequently, our union with Christ "is union with the justified Messiah and the new righteous One."[54]

To put the point slightly differently, on the traditional type of understanding, the death of Christ is the sufficient basis for our justification whether or not Christ is subsequently raised from the dead. The resurrection then is in danger of being nothing more than a public demonstration that Christ's death was effective, a sort of sermon in action. On the view that is being developed here, the Pauline teaching is that the death by itself is not sufficient to justify us without the verdict of God expressed in his carrying into effect the result of Christ's death, namely the pardon and enlivening of the sinner who is now brought into the new life of the justified.

The theological significance of Romans 4:25

Some significant corollaries follow from this understanding.

Substitution and representation

First, it follows that, in the event of crucifixion and resurrection, it is inadequate to think of Christ purely as substitute. Substitution means that Christ acts instead of us,[55] and does something that, as a result of his doing it, we do not need to do. We do *not* have to bear the eternal consequences of our sin because Christ has done so.[56] But the same cannot be said of resurrection. Christ is not raised instead of us, but so that we might share his resurrection. He is raised for us, for

---

[54] Bird, "Justified," 88.

[55] It is something that we cannot do for ourselves, and, therefore, we need somebody to stand in as our substitute, but that is not the point at issue here.

[56] Hooker, *Paul*, 92, insists that Christ's death for us is not substitutionary in regard to physical death or death to sin, both of which we must undergo. This is correct but it does not take into account the fact that Christ bore the consequences of sin, the wrath of God, and eternal exclusion from his presence, so that we shall not have to bear them. It is this latter aspect which is unambiguously substitutionary.

our benefit, on our behalf, in order that what has happened in him may be recapitulated in us, by what has happened in him being extended to us as we are joined to him by faith.

Consequently, those theologians have a point who assert that representative is the more inclusive term than substitute; substitution is a valid, necessary, and essential category to cover that which Christ does for us so that we do not have to do it, but some such term as representation is necessary to cover that which Christ does for us so that we may share in it.[57] God does something to Christ that is extended to those who are represented by him; compare how a king might make a symbolic presentation of a gift to a representative of his subjects, and the gift is then enjoyed by them all. The danger arises when theologians use the term representation because they do not want to talk of substitution. Alternatively, it may be helpful to think of Christ as the one in whom we are incorporated or with whom we are identified or in whom (or better, in whose situation) we participate.

Participation and incorporation in Christ

Romans 6 speaks about believers being baptized into Christ and, hence, into his death. Although Paul develops this aspect of his thought primarily in order to indicate that believers should not remain in sin but rather have the power to overcome its appeal to them, in fact, it reveals the underlying rationale of his soteriology. Believers are united with Christ. This is expressed in their baptism, which Paul understands as a baptism into Christ's death. He does not speak of their baptism as being a baptism into Christ's resurrection. This is probably because baptism is understood as symbolizing death, in line with the well-known metaphorical use of being plunged into, or deluged with, water. Death delivers the person from sin, meaning deliverance from its captivity which includes receiving its wages, namely death. But, by Christ's death, the believer is regarded as having died and, therefore, no longer being under the domination of sin. But

---

[57] Forsyth, P. T. *The Work of Christ*. London: Independent Press, 1938[2], 182.

that can only be half the story. In the case of Jesus, he is resurrected from the dead. He has died once and for all from sin. Now he lives the new life of those who have been raised by God, and it is this life that is shared with believers who are united with him. Thus union with Christ by faith means that believers share in what we can rightly call the justification of Christ as the representative of sinners. They now share in his life, and they are in effect spiritually resurrected with Christ, as the clear statements in Ephesians 2:5–6 and Colossians 2:12–13 indicate.

Other New Testament modes of expression

Hebrews. We can now take a step forward and claim that what Paul is expressing in this way is complementary to what is expressed in Hebrews. In Hebrews, Christ's death as sacrifice is followed by his (resurrection and) entry into heaven to present that sacrifice to God. What we saw as surprisingly absent from Hebrews is any statement that the offering is actually accepted by God. That is taken for granted. Romans, however, sees God's acceptance of the sacrifice as taking place in the resurrection of Jesus and in the intercession that follows. It is emphasized that it is God who justifies sinners (Rom. 8:33; cf. 3:26). Thus Romans and Hebrews offer complementary insights that together enable us to grasp more fully the significance of the resurrection and ascension.

Luke-Acts. In the light of this, the soteriology in Acts merits a fresh examination. The resurrection is here the means by which God exalts Jesus and appoints him to be Lord and Messiah, a Leader and Savior (Luke 24:26; Acts 3:13; 5:31). Thus a positive value is assigned to the action of resurrection. It is certainly a reversal of what wicked men have done and, to that extent, a vindication of Jesus to the world, but it is also a cosmic vindication of Jesus, because, in this action, God now seats Jesus beside him as the giver of salvation.[58]

---

[58] The term "cosmic" requires some defense. The reference is to an event that takes place before heavenly spectators (cf. 1 Tim. 3:16) and which

The thought of affirming what Jesus did on the cross may not be so apparent. Yet it remains the case that the death of Jesus, though brought about by evil men, is nevertheless something that was planned and purposed by God: the Messiah had to suffer, and then enter into glory. But why was the suffering necessary? It may well be that commentators have generally attached too little significance to Luke 22:37. It is common to deny any vicarious sense in this text. This is partly because it is urged that this line of thought is not developed elsewhere in Luke-Acts, and that this sense is not required by the present text, which is simply stating that it is Jesus' lot to be treated like a lawless person, with the implication that his followers will be treated similarly. L. Morris, by contrast, says: "Jesus sees his death as one in which he will be one with sinners. This surely points to that death as substitutionary: Jesus will take the place of sinful people."[59] Hence this statement, drawn as it is from the Servant-prophecy in Isaiah 53, and occurring not many verses after the sayings at the Last Supper, may well have a secondary force that there was a divine purpose in Jesus' death which went beyond simply providing an occasion for God to raise him from the dead. In any case, the thought of Christ dying for sinners is present in the sayings at the Last Supper (Luke 22:19–20).[60]

Even without this thought, it remains the case that the resurrection is the glorification of Jesus as the Messiah, and this is rather more than simply vindicating the one who was

---

is known by faith to God's people on earth; for them, in the light of scriptural references to the exaltation of the Messiah, the attestation of Jesus' resurrection to his followers in the empty tomb and the appearances was proof of the heavenly exaltation of Jesus and, consequently, of his divine vindication.

[59] Morris, L. *Luke: An Introduction and Commentary.* Leicester: IVP, 1988[2], 339. Other commentators tend to deny that there is any explicit substitutionary reference here.

[60] However, the authenticity of Luke 22:19b–20 continues to be debated. For a recent negative verdict, see McKnight, S. *Jesus and His Death: Historiography, the Historical Jesus, and Atonement Theory.* Waco, TX: Baylor University Press, 2005, 260 n. 4. Nor should we forget Acts 20:28 where the blood of Christ plays a decisive role in the creation of the new people of God.

crucified as a malefactor. It is his enthronement as Messiah. So, for Luke-Acts, the resurrection and exaltation has the character of a saving event, the enthronement of Jesus as Leader and Savior.

The thought in Paul goes further, in that Jesus is vindicated as the representative righteous One in whom his people are accepted by God. Nevertheless, common to Paul and Luke is the belief that in raising Jesus from the dead God *makes* him the one through whom salvation is conferred and does not merely publicly acknowledge him as such.

1 Peter. Similar things might be said about 1 Peter, where both cross and resurrection figure prominently. Here there is no question but that the suffering and death of Jesus on behalf of the unjust, bearing their sins, is clearly taught; then Peter elaborates that Christ was put to death in the flesh but made alive in the spirit. Of particular significance for our purpose is the statement that baptism now saves through the resurrection of Jesus (1 Pet. 3:18, 21; cf. 1:3, 21; 2:24). The precise way in which the resurrection functions in relation to the death of Jesus is not spelled out. But the way in which the resurrection is referred to suggests that it is more than simply ratification or evidence of the saving power of the death, but is itself an integral part of the total saving event. Since the purpose of Christ was to bring sinners to God, his resurrection should be seen as the means by which this takes place.

Paradox and mystery

There are various paradoxes in this understanding of things.

The death of Jesus is the death of the Son of God,[61] and not the death of the Father.[62] Equally, the resurrection is the resurrection of Jesus as man and as Son of God. There is

---

[61] The death is specifically the death of the Son, Romans 5:10 (8:32); Galatians 2:20; implied in Philippians 2:6–8; 1 John 1:7; 4:10; John 3:16; 8:35; Hebrews 6:6. So is the resurrection, 1 Thessalonians 1:10.

[62] The hymns of Isaac Watts and Charles Wesley emphasize that it is Jesus Christ as Son of God, himself God, who hangs on the cross and dies.

no suggestion that God the Father dies. We thus have, from our later point of view, the paradox of one member of the Trinity dying (and being raised) but not the others. We have the further paradox that the Son of God is capable of death. A solution to these mysteries must take seriously the incarnation of the Son of God as a human being, for whom death is a possibility and reality. This is clearly taught in Philippians 2:6–9, although Paul does not stop to consider how it was possible. Neither the Father nor the Spirit became incarnate.

The language of intercession and offering envisages the Son requesting pardon for sinners from the Father; nevertheless, the sacrifice and offering are initiated by the Father in his grace, and, according to Romans 4:25, he has raised Jesus in order that sinners may be justified. There is no doubt, therefore, about the outcome of Christ's intercession. While it could be the case that the Son is portrayed as acting with God in his capacity as a human being on behalf of human beings, nevertheless it is specifically as Son that he intercedes (Rom. 8:34, in light of 8:32; 1 John 2:1, in light of 1:7; Heb. 7:25, in light of 7:28). Moreover, the gracious saving purpose of God the Father is apparent; note how the love of Christ in Romans 8:35 slides into the love of God in Christ Jesus our Lord in 8:39. The imagery functions to provide both a way for believers to approach the Father on the basis of the One who died for them, and an assurance that the sacrifice that he offered avails for ever. Thus all believers share in the priesthood of Christ, in the sense that they have access through and in him to God.[63]

Conclusion

What has emerged from this discussion of the contributions of various recent scholars, who have revived an insight from an earlier generation, is a persuasive interpretation of Romans 4:25 that integrates Jesus' resurrection into the saving event

---

[63] No special priesthood of some believers (ordained ministers) is needed.

on the basis of which we are justified. Jesus Christ, who died bearing our sins and atoning for them, is released from death by God the Father; he has done representatively what was needed for sinful humanity so as to uphold the holiness and righteousness of God. So he is representatively justified in order that those who believe and are joined to him by baptism into his death may share in his representative justification, and enter into the new life that has been conferred on him by the Father. Thus the raising of Jesus by God the Father is seen to be an essential part of the saving act, and is not simply a way of proclaiming to humanity that the price of sin has been paid. If Christ had not been raised, we would still be in our sins. This way of understanding the significance of the resurrection for Paul corresponds to the reality expressed in a somewhat different imagery in Hebrews, 1 Peter and Luke-Acts. Moreover, it explains how it is that on occasion the New Testament writers can depict the resurrection and exaltation of Jesus as the saving event without explicit reference to his death.

4 Reconciliation:
Its Centrality and Relevance

The theme of the 19th World Methodist Conference meeting in Seoul in 2006 was "God in Christ Reconciling." The title was chosen by the Korean Church which longs to see the reunification of the Korean peninsula and lasting peace between the two divided nations of North and South Korea. Back in 2004 in Cambridge at a special service held to commemorate the 500th anniversary of the establishment of Lady Margaret's Preachership in the University, Professor G. N. Stanton took as the theme of his sermon "Terrorism and Reconciliation."[1] These two examples from opposite sides of the world indicate the timeliness of the theme to be addressed in this final installment of a series devoted to significant aspects of the saving work of Christ. In the previous three chapters, we have been looking at how the work of Christ effects atonement. Now, in this final chapter, we shall consider how we understand the effects of that atoning action.

There have been some major discussions about reconciliation in the New Testament in recent scholarship, as a result of which, certain aspects of the doctrine seem to me to be reasonably established. My interest in the present paper is twofold. I want to consider the related issues of the place of the doctrine in the New Testament, and its relevance for the witness of the Christian church at the present time.

The mending of relationships both with God and with our fellow human beings is a central theme in the New Testament, and especially in the writings of Paul. Romans is concerned to

---

[1] Stanton, G. N. "Terrorism and Reconciliation." *Theology* 108 (no. 845; Sept/Oct 2005): 331-337.

bring together Jewish and Gentile believers in praise of God; 1 Corinthians deals with a church that is split into groups over personalities and spiritual gifts; 2 Corinthians deals with a rift in the church between some of its members and Paul, and between two rival Christian missions; Galatians has the problem of fellowship between Jewish and Gentile Christians as its underlying concern; Ephesians makes the unity of the church thematic; Philippians is written to encourage the members of the church to be united in their concern for one another, and in standing up to external pressures; 1 Thessalonians commends the readers for their mutual love; Philemon deals with the relationship between a master and a slave. The frequency and centrality of the issue is obvious.

The place of the doctrine

Let me begin with a contrast in scholarship. On the one hand, we have two leading New Testament scholars who assign a central place to reconciliation in New Testament theology.

First, there is the German theologian P. Stuhlmacher. Over many years he has insisted on this point, stating (for example): "The formation of the New Testament tradition [will have] the proclamation of Jesus Christ as Messianic Reconciler [as] its genuinely theological and critical center."[2] In his recent, definitive study of New Testament theology, he faces the criticism that it is inadmissible to place a theme that occurs only in Paul, and there only sporadically, at the centre of a biblical theology of the New Testament, and he reiterates that it marks the soteriological centre of Scripture. Later in his book, he justifies this thesis in more detail.[3]

Second, the proposal was developed in a book-length study by R. P. Martin that appeared exactly twenty-five years ago.

---

[2] Stuhlmacher, P. *Historical Criticism and Theological Interpretation of Scripture: Towards a Hermeneutic of Consent.* Philadelphia, PA: Fortress, 1977, 90-91, cited by Martin, R. P. *Reconciliation: A Study of Paul's Theology.* Atlanta, GA.: John Knox Press/London: Marshall, Morgan and Scott, 1981, 3.

[3] Stuhlmacher, P. *Biblische Theologie des Neuen Testaments.* Göttingen: Vandenhoeck und Ruprecht, 1992, 1999, I, 32–33. Cf. II, 320–321.

The title, *Reconciliation: A Study of Paul's Theology*, indicates that Martin is concerned with the more limited task of arguing that reconciliation is the centre of Pauline theology. It is the key motif in the theology of Paul, the central theme which could serve as an organizing principle for his theology. Martin summarizes his discussion by stating that he has been looking for the "leading theme" or "centre" of Paul's teaching. None of the previous attempts satisfy him. "We really need a larger frame to encompass the apostle's diverse modes of expression. It is for this reason that Paul's thought can best be captured in the omnibus term 'reconciliation.'" The advantages of this choice listed by Martin are: 1. It expresses the cosmic predicament in terms of estrangement from God. 2. The saving action of God is leading to a universe at one with its creator. Barriers of separation between humankind and between groups in society are being broken down. 3. Paul's own experience set the pattern for his thinking. His theology is essentially relational.[4]

But now, on the other hand, consider what happens, or rather doesn't happen, in the fullest contemporary English reference work on the Bible, the *Anchor Bible Dictionary*, a work running to six volumes, each of over 1000 pp. With 6000 pp. to play with, the compilers could evidently find no room in volume 5, in between entries on such central themes of the Bible as "Rechabites" and "Recorder" (p. 633), for any mention of reconciliation; there is not even a cross-reference to some other article that would include the topic. Yes, "Redemption" is covered; so too is "Atonement" in a rather broad sweep covering 5 pp. and including one paragraph headed "Reconciliation"(I, 521), but otherwise we shall hunt in vain for mention of this theme.[5]

Childs, B. S. *Biblical Theology of the Old and New Testaments: Theological Reflection on the Christian Bible.* Minneapolis, MN: Fortress, 1992, 485–531, also regards reconciliation as "a broad inclusive theological category" that "encompasses the subject matter of atonement, sacrifice, forgiveness, redemption, righteousness and justification" (486); under this heading he discusses righteousness, atonement, and victory, but strangely does not discuss reconciliation as such, nor does he really attempt to show how the subcategories are integrally related to the concept of reconciliation.
[4] Martin, *Reconciliation*, 46–47.
[5] There is no article on the biblical term "mediator."

Even in confessedly evangelical publications, where you would expect to find particular attention devoted to the subject, the coverage is slight. One recent dictionary treats it along with "Forgiveness," but it is forgiveness that gets the major share of the coverage. Another treats it under "Peace."[6] It scarcely figures in the index of the most recent monograph on New Testament theology.[7]

In the light of the marginalization of this theme in major reference works, it may seem ludicrous to argue for it as a candidate for a central position in New Testament theology. Nevertheless, the attempt is worth making.

At the outset we need to be clear what we are looking for. Some distinctions may be helpful.

First, a theme may be central to the whole New Testament or merely to some part of it. Martin's concern was simply to demonstrate that reconciliation is central to Pauline theology, but it seems that Stuhlmacher's aim is to show that it is central to all New Testament theology, or even to biblical theology.

Second, to look for a central, unifying theme assumes that a writer (or speaker) has a coherent outlook rather than a collection of unrelated or inconsistent ideas. This is not to say that everything will necessarily fit together or be directly related to the central theme, but that, on the whole, this is the case. We are examining the unifying theme within a particular field, rather than what a writer may say in discussions of different areas. We would not necessarily expect to find a common theme across one and the same journalist's treatments of sport and science fiction.

---

[6] Yarbrough R. W. In *New Dictionary of Biblical Theology*, edited by T. D. Alexander and B. S. Rosner. Leicester/Downers Grove: IVP, 2000, 498–503; Porter S. E. In *Dictionary of Paul and his Letters*, edited by G. F. Hawthorne, R. P. Martin and D. G. Reid. Downers Grove/Leicester: IVP, 1993, 695–699.

[7] Thielman, F. *Theology of the New Testament: a canonical and synthetic approach.* Grand Rapids, MI: Zondervan, 2005, 387, 691; in neither reference is the topic developed to any extent. Cf. Moo, D. *The Epistle to the Romans.* Grand Rapids, MI: Eerdmans, 1996, 297 n. 20, who cites, with approval, the opinion of E. Käsemann and concludes "It is better to view reconciliation as one image, among many others, that is used to capture something of the meaning of God's act in Christ for us."

Third, consider, as an example, the question about whether or not the teaching of Jesus in the Synoptic Gospels has some kind of center. It would be possible to argue that the unifying theme is the revelation of God as Father, and then to attempt to see the various things that Jesus says as facets of this theme. But it is also arguable that the concept of the kingdom of God is in fact more of a basic theme than God as Father, even though this latter concept also underlies all that Jesus teaches. Jesus comes, announcing: "The kingdom of God has drawn near" rather than "God is our Father." It is a question of enunciating what is of central importance, perhaps even what is distinctive, an organizing principle that enables us to fit together, in a coherent manner, the details of what is said.

Fourth, the center may be a complex of ideas, rather than one simple one. "Kingdom of God" needs some unpacking before it can serve as a satisfactory description of what is central to the teaching of Jesus.

Fifth, even within the same book (or author) there may be different levels at which centrality can be investigated. Thus, although I am suggesting that the central theme of the teaching of Jesus, as reported by any of the Synoptic Evangelists, is the kingdom of God, it is also the case that the central theme of the Evangelists themselves is Jesus and "all that he began both to do and to teach," rather than simply what he taught.

Sixth, similarly, a distinction might be made between the theology and soteriology of the documents. Thus it could be argued that "reconciliation" is central in the soteriology, whereas the theology is centered on Jesus Christ. One or two scholars find the central theme of the New Testament and, indeed of the Bible, to be the glory or glorification of God, rather than the salvation of lost humanity, but this seems to me to confuse an ultimate goal with the means to that end, and the latter is developed more fully.

Finally, it is very important to recognize that we are talking about a concept. This not the same thing as a vocabulary item or group which is frequently in use (though "kingdom of God" fits this bill for Jesus). In the particular case of reconciliation, we may be thinking of an idea that may be expressed in various ways without use of the specific word-group or word-groups that clearly refer to it.

What I am proposing that we look for, therefore, is whether there is some central idea that expresses the soteriology of Paul, namely what is achieved by the work of Christ, so that the main lines of Paul's teaching can be seen as the working out of this basic concept, rather than as different, diverse, possibly even mutually contradictory lines of thought. Then we will consider whether, if there is such a central idea, it can be regarded as having a similar, central role elsewhere in the New Testament. I shall conclude by noting one aspect of the practical, contemporary relevance of the doctrine.

Thematic treatments of reconciliation in the Pauline letters

The theme of divine-human reconciliation comes clearly to the surface in a set of passages that specifically use the word-group (*katallassō, apokatallassō*).

In 2 Corinthians 5:17-21, Paul moves from the thought of a new creation to that of reconciliation. Prior to their conversion, God had credited the readers with their offences. Now he has made Christ to be sin for them, with the result that their sins need no longer be held against them, and harmony between God and people is possible. This good news has been entrusted to God's messengers so that they can proclaim the openness of the amnesty that is available, and people can be reconciled to God. Two points are significant. One is the fact that the concept of enmity as the state from which deliverance is needed is not used in this passage. The thought is rather of sin and trespasses. Thus there is a close link to the language of justification. The second feature is the thematizing of the need to proclaim reconciliation alongside the prior act of reconciliation in Christ.

In Romans 5:10–11, Paul uses the concept of reconciliation to back up what he says about justification.[8] He concludes his

---

[8] The thought of reconciliation is already present in Romans 5:1 where

discussion of justification as a present experience of believers, by saying that, if God has justified sinners by the blood of Christ, they can be certain that, now that they have been justified, they will be delivered from his wrath at the last judgement. Similarly, those who once were his enemies, but have now been reconciled by his Son's death, can be sure that they will be saved by his Son's life. Here, a previous situation of sin and enmity is envisaged. The enmity is best understood as mutual. But, despite his enmity, God, in his love, acted to provide a means whereby sin and its consequences could be canceled, and he could treat people as friends rather than enemies; this involved Christ dying for them. The intended readers of the letter have thus been reconciled to God, and they are now destined for final salvation. It might be claimed that here reconciliation is brought in, at a secondary stage, to back up what has been said about the primary concept of justification, but one might equally well say that reconciliation is the climax of this section.

In Colossians 1:19–23,[9] there are two stages in Paul's presentation. First, he describes God's act of reconciliation through Christ, specifically through his death on the cross, which is effective on a cosmic scale and covers "all things" on earth and in heaven. Verse 23 makes it clear that Paul is thinking primarily of the fact that this provides the basis for the other essential part of the saving action, the preaching of the gospel throughout the world to everybody. Second, this cosmic event is particularized with reference to the readers; they were alienated from God and treated him as their enemy, but have now been reconciled through Jesus' death

---

the result of justification is peace with God and access into a relationship based on grace.

[9] I am persuaded by the arguments of those who defend the Pauline authorship of both Colossians and Ephesians, but I do not think that my case is in any way dependent upon this conclusion. For Colossians, see Dunn, J. D. G. *The Epistles to the Colossians and to Philemon*. Grand Rapids, MI: Eerdmans/Carlisle: Paternoster Press, 1996 (possibly indirect through Timothy); O'Brien, P. T. *Colossians, Philemon*. Waco, TX: Word Books, 1982; for Ephesians, see Hoehner, H. W. *Ephesians: An Exegetical Commentary*. Grand Rapids, MI: Baker, 2002.

so that they may be holy and blameless before God. Faith is implied in Romans 5:1 as the basis for reconciliation; it is also implied in 2 Corinthians 5, where there is reference to receiving the grace of God. Here in Colossians, Paul explicitly refers to continuation in the faith which is the response to the gospel that the Colossian believers have heard. Note again the reference to the preaching of reconciliation as an essential part of the process.

In Ephesians 2, Paul begins with a description of how God saved those who were sinners (and, as such, dead) by raising them. Earlier in the epistle, he had described them as having received redemption that consists in the forgiveness of sins by the blood of Christ. Now he goes on to speak particularly of the readers as Gentiles who had formerly been alienated both from the people of God and from God's covenants, but who have now been brought near by the blood of Christ, through an action which makes Jews and Gentiles into one people of God. Here the thought of becoming part of the people of God is tied in with reconciliation to God himself. To be reconciled with God is the same thing as becoming part of his people. Hence the hostility that is destroyed is between Gentiles and Jews, as well as between both of them and God. Jews need to be reconciled with Gentiles and Gentiles with Jews as an integral part of their reconciliation with God. To sum up:

1. In all four passages, reconciliation is treated explicitly and thematically.
2. Together the passages offer a coherent and harmonious doctrine:
   • They picture human beings as enemies of God through their sins.
   • God acts in Christ to reconcile them to himself through his death.
   • What God has done is then proclaimed in the world, and reconciliation is made between God and those who accept the message in faith.
   • Those who are reconciled now enjoy peace with God and are included in his holy people.

- In Ephesians and Colossians, the reconciliation specifically includes the ending of the enmity between Jews and Gentiles in the new people of God.
- There is an obligation laid upon the reconciled people to proclaim God's action in the world.

3. The use of the terminology is confined to Paul (or to Paul and his followers).

This may seem to be a very limited basis for claiming the centrality of the motif of reconciliation in Pauline theology. But we are exploring a concept and not just a single word-group. Two other closely-connected word-groups should be brought in to fill out the picture.[10] They give us a fuller understanding of what is meant by reconciliation, and, at the same time, the breadth of the usage demonstrates that the ideas conveyed by Paul's specialized vocabulary are much more widespread in his writings and in the rest of the New Testament. These other two closely connected word-groups are "peace" and "forgiveness."[11]

---

[10] A third possible candidate for exposition at this point is mediation. The term "mediator" can be used either for a middle-man who comes in between two hostile parties to persuade both of them to abandon their hostility and be at peace, or for a representative sent by one party to negotiate peace with the other. The use of the term is very limited in the New Testament. We can pass over Galatians 3:19-20 where the reference is presumably to Moses conveying God's laws to the people and there is no indication of an analogous role for Christ. In Hebrews the term is used three times of the mediator of a covenant, in each case with reference to Jesus initiating the new covenant and acting on behalf of God to do so (Heb. 8:6; 9:15; 12:24). In 1 Timothy 2:5, Jesus is the one mediator between God and humanity. The use of this language, which suggests the middle-man, may be to do justice to the fact that Jesus acts as a human being in laying down his life on behalf of other human beings as their representative and substitute. Yet, in Titus 2:13-14, it is as the divine Savior that he lays down his life for humanity. In any case, the use of the term evokes the concept of reconciliation as the result of the mediation. In the case of Hebrews. the establishment of the covenant creates a community which is in a harmonious relationship with God.

[11] Reconciliation and forgiveness are assigned to the same word domain in Louw J. P., and E. A. Nida, *Greek-English Lexicon of the New Testament based on Semantic Domains*. New York, NY: United Bible Societies, 1988, I,

Peace

The vocabulary of "peace" is much more common than that of "reconciliation," The word-group is found approximately one hundred times in the NT (in fact, in every book except 1 John). These statistics, however, may be misleading in view of the broad range of meaning attached to the notion, extending beyond the state resulting from reconciliation between enemies. The links with reconciliation are clear in Acts 7:26, and also in Romans 8:5-6, where the peace associated with the mind controlled by the Spirit is contrasted with the enmity towards God displayed by the sinful mind. The connection is most explicit in Colossians 1:20, where the act of reconciliation is identified with the making of peace through the blood of the cross.

Peace is seen as a desirable state in human relationships, both on the personal and the national levels. It includes the inner feeling of calmness and absence of worry that comes about when there is a lack of disturbance. It is largely defined by its opposite, war and strife, with all their undesirable accompaniments.

There is thus a widespread use of the term peace as a broad term for what is covered by our English comprehensive term "salvation"; it is a summary word for the benefits that God confers on those who respond to the gospel with faith.

The choice of the term was doubtless influenced by two factors.

First, there was the secular propaganda regarding the Pax Romana, the peace of a sort that came about through the Roman Empire for which the Roman emperors claimed the credit. This ensured the relative absence of foreign foes from Roman soil, and the conditions in which at least some people could enjoy prosperity and freedom from worry. One can rightly be cynical about it. Calgacus, the earliest Scottish nationalist of whom we have evidence, is credited by Tacitus with the succinct statement "they create a wilderness

---

502–504. "Peace-making" is included in the same domain, but not "peace" itself.

and they call it peace" ("ubi solitudinem faciunt, pacem appellant").[12]

Second, we have the Old Testament background where *shalom* expresses in a broad manner the blessed situation that God confers on his people. It is generally agreed that this is the dominant influence on the thought of the New Testament. The choice of this word is accordingly well-justified. It includes the thought of reconciliation as part of peace-making, but it also includes the forceful quelling of those who disturb the peace. In the Christian context, such peace is associated with God's presence and is an on-going consequence of that presence. The association of peace with grace emphasizes that it is rooted in the loving character of God, and must be seen as something that he gives or brings about.

Peace in the Gospels

Of the Evangelists, it is Luke who makes greatest use of the vocabulary. In Mark, the vocabulary of peace occurs only twice. Once it appears in the conclusion to a healing story (the woman with a hemorrhage, Mark 5:34) and then in an instruction to disciples not to quarrel (cf. Mark 9:34 with 9:50). Matthew has neither statement, but has the blessing on those who make peace in Matthew 5:9 (followed by the pericope about making peace before offering sacrifice, and the command to forgive one another in the Lord's Prayer), and then the two Q statements, one about offering peace during mission (Matt. 10:13), and the other about the fact that Jesus did not come to bring peace on earth, but a sword (Matt. 10:34).

A surprising contrast is provided by Luke who has the word fourteen times in his Gospel.[13] Peace appears in a

---

[12] Tacitus, *Agricola*, 30.

[13] There are also seven occurrences in Acts. However, the only soteriological usage is in Acts 10:36; there is one reference to the peace enjoyed for a period by the church in Acts 9:31. Other references are mundane: one is about bringing a quarrel to an end (Acts 7:26); two are political (Acts 12:20; 24:2) ; and a further two refer to people parting from one another on good terms (Acts 16:36 and 15:33).

number of programmatic statements. In Luke 2:14, the birth of Jesus into the world is heralded by the angels announcing peace on earth for the people on whom his favor rests and glory to God in the highest places; the birth of the Messiah is associated with peace on earth. (Compare how the child in Isaiah 9:6 who is the prince of peace acts peaceably and so produces peace.) Similarly, and somewhat surprisingly, in Luke 19:38 the coming of Jesus into Jerusalem is accompanied by the crowds saying: "peace in heaven and glory in the highest places." (This should not be taken to deny that peace is available on earth for those who welcome Jesus; Jesus weeps because people did not recognize their opportunity [Luke 19:42]).

The song of Zechariah announces that the purpose of God is to guide our feet into the way of peace (Luke 1:79). This verse may reflect Isaiah 59:8: evil-doers and violent people do not know the way of peace and there is no justice in their paths (cf. the citation in Rom. 3:17). These people of whom Isaiah was speaking do not do the things that promote peace but rather cause strife, violence and resulting harm, and they do not act justly in accordance with divine norms of conduct. Here in Luke, however, the people in mind are in darkness and the shadow of death as the victims of others (cf. Luke 1:71, 74). God's purpose is to direct them into ways that will lead them to experience peace. The way of peace is a complex of actions that promote peace and the resulting conditions; it leads to peace and is characterized by peace.

Simeon is able to die serenely in a situation of peace with God, with no worries about the future, whether for the world he leaves behind or for himself (Luke 2:29). All is well. Why? Because God is acting for salvation. Peace is the human experience arising from salvation. Likewise, in Acts, Peter announces to Cornelius that God was announcing the good news of peace through Jesus (Acts 10:36; cf. Eph. 2:17).

Even if these statements stood alone, they would make a fair case that, for Luke, the principal effect of Jesus' coming is to make peace possible. The statements are, of course, accompanied by others which indicate that salvation is at least an equally central and important category. In all these cases, it is arguable that the peace is a gift to those who are oppressed by their enemies, not an offer of reconciliation to the enemies themselves.

The Gospels contain what could be a stereotyped usage. Jesus uses the introductory greeting "peace be with you" (Luke 24:36; John 20:19, 21, 26) and the farewell greeting "go in peace" (Mark 5:34; Luke 7:50; 8:48; Acts 16:36; cf. Acts 15:33) in a variety of situations. But the fact that these standard forms are deliberately quoted by the Evangelists probably indicates that there is a deeper significance when Jesus (or his disciples) uses them, that they are not simply formal but should be taken seriously.

So the outcome of healing and forgiveness is that a person can go away with inner peace and calm; a cause of disturbance has been removed (Mark 5:34; Luke 7:50; 8:48).

The element of freedom from war or bringing war to an end is not conspicuous here, although it is inherent in the introductory greetings which convey the sense "you have nothing to fear from me." Reference to war is explicit in the statement that Jesus did not come to bring peace but a sword, a reference to the opposition that disciples can expect to face (Matt. 10:34). Paradoxically, there can be a deeper peace in this situation in that. Although there may be opposition on a human and satanic level, nevertheless, nothing can disturb the positive relationship with God.

As for the farewell "Go in peace," this concludes an encounter in which the participants are in or have entered into harmony with Jesus. They can, therefore, depart, knowing that there is no cause for fear, and, indeed, they go with Jesus' blessing.[14] All of this presupposes a state of harmony and lack of hostility; the greeting is not so much an offer of reconciliation as rather an indication that a state of reconciliation has been established.

---

[14] The wording indicates that it is the person who (at least temporarily) stays put who expresses the wish, rather than those who are departing. The notable exception to this direction of the blessing is when the departing Jesus in Luke 24:36 and John 14:27 expresses peace to those whom he leaves behind, but there he is returning to what might be regarded as his home.

Alongside this, we have the introductory usage on occasions when evangelists visiting homes wish peace to those living in them (Luke 10:5–6 par. Matt. 10:13; cf. Jesus himself in John 20:19, 21, 26). This cannot simply be a formal greeting, otherwise there would be no point in mentioning something that would be taken for granted. The function of the words is probably twofold: to assure the people visited that they have nothing to fear from the visitors and to express an implicit prayer for God's blessing on them. Presumably then, the appropriate response must be more than the politeness and courtesy that could perhaps be taken for granted. This is seen from the reference to a householder who is a person of peace (Luke 10:6).[15] Here we have a receptive person who is destined for peace or worthy of peace, somebody looking for peace, who welcomes the messengers. The implied contrast is with the people of Jerusalem who do not recognize what will bring them to peace and so reject the messenger. The consequence of this rejection is judgement which is expressed in the familiar pattern of OT siege and death. Thus peace is understood very concretely in contrast to war and its awful effects.

Whereas, in Paul, the offer of reconciliation is to those who create the hostility and mayhem, the Gospel usage is concerned in general with the bringing of peace and its blessings to the oppressed. Nevertheless, it conveys the message of a God who offers peace and not war to the people, and it is thus broadly concerned with reconciliation.

Peace in Paul

The opening greetings in most of the New Testament letters extend a wish for grace and peace to the recipients; the combination is a fixed one, sometimes expanded by the addition of mercy. Because of the formal nature of these greetings it is easy to underestimate their significance. Such a greeting occurs in every Pauline letter and also in the majority of the other New Testament letters.[16] It also occurs

---

[15] This formulation is peculiar to Luke's version.

[16] Including the greeting in Revelation; the exceptions are James (secular greeting); Hebrews; 1 John and 3 John which do not have a greeting.

in five closing benedictions (Gal. 6:16; Eph. 6:23; 2 Thess. 3:16; 1 Pet. 5:14; 3 John 15). These are all expressed in the form of wishes that may be understood as prayers[17] or perhaps as statements of what the writer expects to be the case (so explicitly in 2 John 3). This understanding rests on the fact that the grace and peace come from God and Jesus Christ.

Although the language may appear to have become stereotyped, the variety of expression found, especially in the benedictions, shows that the form is still very much alive and open to creative use. This vitality appears in the several references to the God of peace, i.e., the God who is the source of peace. Thus, the God of peace is said to be with people (Rom. 15:33; 2 Cor. 13:11; Phil. 4:9), and Paul prays that the God of peace will give peace (2 Thess. 3:16). When Paul says that the God of peace will bruise Satan (Rom. 16:20), it is fair to conclude that it is the quelling of Satan by God that leads to peace for the readers.

The vitality of the concept is further seen in the other examples of Pauline usage. Four specific points should be noticed:

1. Peace is frequently used as an all-encompassing term for salvation. The gospel announces and conveys peace, even though the imagery in which it occurs is that of the warrior church armed for its struggle with the powers of darkness (Eph. 6:15). But there is nothing untoward here, for the weapons of warfare are spiritual (2 Cor. 10:4) and the contest is one of spiritual victory over these powers in order to bring about the peace and rule of God. Paul sees peace as the gift of God to his people, along with glory and honor (Rom. 2:10). It might perhaps be understood as eschatological reward.[18]

2. The concept of peace is used, in a broad sense, to refer to what God creates for those oppressed by their enemies; to

---

[17] This is explicit in the greetings where a verb is present, 1 Peter 1:2; 2 Peter 1:2.

[18] Here the concept is not tied closely to reconciliation except in the broad sense that, in the kingdom of God, strife is absent and peace is practiced.

a lesser extent, it refers to the making of peace between God and those who are hostile to him. Yet the boundaries between these types of usage are so vague that the concept of reconciliation and harmony between God and people who rebel against him is fairly widely present.

3. In a number of texts, the term "enmity" functions to describe the situation before peace was brought about (Rom. 5:10; 8:7; 11:28; Eph. 2:14, 16; Phil. 3:18; Col. 1:21; Jas. 4:4). There is considerable support for the view that this term refers primarily to "the objective state of enmity which, in consequence of sins, existed between [God] and men."[19] The enmity is that which exists between God and the people to whom he offers peace and not that between them and other people or forces who oppress them. Thus, in Ephesians 2:1–12, the readers are described as children of wrath and disobedience, people who were once far from God, "without God in the world," and thus in a state of alienation from him. God's own action in Christ changes the situation where he is hostile or judgemental towards sinners with one of harmony and love. Peace is made through the blood of the cross, by which enmity is slain (Col. 1:20; Eph. 2:16). Here, then, peace, elsewhere described as the fruit of justification (Rom. 5:1),[19] is closely associated with reconciliation.

4. Paul also sees peace, i.e., peaceableness, as the fruit of the Spirit (Rom. 8:6; 14:17, 19; Gal. 5:22). The line between experiencing peace (Phil. 4:7) and being a person who acts peaceably is hard to draw (cf. Rom. 15:13; Eph. 4:3; Col. 3:15; cf. elsewhere Jas. 3:18; 1 Pet. 3:11). Those who experience divine peace are called to be agents of that peace to others. The concept of peacemaking used of God in Colossians 1:20 is applied to disciples in Matthew 5:9, and the peace bestowed in Ephesians 2 is, at one and the same time, peace with God and between Jews and Gentiles. Some scholars hold that, throughout the pericope,

---

[19] Bultmann, R. *Theology of the New Testament*. London: SCM Press, 1952, 1953, I, 287. This statement can be made while emphasizing that the initiative for reconciliation comes from God himself who does not need to be propitiated by his enemies before he offers peace to them.

the word "peace" (Eph. 2:14, 15, 17a, 17b) refers simply to the new situation between Jews and Gentiles brought about by Christ rather than peace with God. However, the former interpretation is more probable.

In the rest of the New Testament, peace is admittedly rarely mentioned except in the formulaic statements already mentioned. The only other significant usage is that peace, in the sense of peaceableness, is a quality of believers (Heb. 12:14; Jas. 3:18; 1 Pet. 3:11; cf. 2 Pet. 3:14).

The use of the concept of peace clearly ties in closely with the concept of reconciliation, but it also indicates how the basic concept of the resulting divine-human relationship permeates the New Testament generally. The language of salvation as peace is mainly found in Paul and Luke (with some basis in the tradition of Jesus' teaching). It embraces the ideas of peace and reconciliation with God, the resultant situation of security, tranquility, and well-being, and the development of a peaceable attitude to other people. Elsewhere in the New Testament, it is much less frequent and the focus on reconciliation with God is hardly to be found.

Forgiveness

The other concept with which reconciliation tends to be linked is forgiveness.

In the Gospels the blessing bestowed by John the Baptist is characterized as forgiveness of sins, with John acting as God's agent in bestowing it.[20] Jesus, likewise, forgives sins in his role as Son of Man (Mark 2:1–10). A sinful woman is told that her sins are forgiven, and Jesus comments that a person who is forgiven will love the person who has done the forgiving (Luke 7:36–50). Disciples are told to pray daily for forgiveness, and they are commanded to forgive other people, otherwise God will not forgive them (Matt. 6:12,

---

[20] Mark 1:4; Luke 3:3; cf. 1:77; Matthew omits the term "forgiveness" but the concept is implicit (Matt. 3:6).

14-15; 18:21-35). In Matthew 26:28, the phrase is associated with the shedding of the blood of Jesus.[21]

John the Baptist made a contrast between his own baptizing with water, which led to the forgiveness of sins, and the baptism with the Holy Spirit by the Messiah. It is significant, however, that proclamation of the Messiah by his evangelists incorporates forgiveness in the offer of salvation, and the rite of baptism with water was maintained. Forgiveness and the gift of the Spirit constitute salvation in the early church (Luke 24:47; Acts 2:38; 5:31; 10:43; 13:38 and 26:18). In line with this, John, in his Gospel, tells how the disciples are to forgive sins on behalf of God after Jesus' resurrection (John 20:23). So it is not surprising that forgiveness figures prominently in 1 John 1:9; 2:12. James associates forgiveness with prayer for healing of the sick (Jas. 5:15).

Forgiveness is an integral part of redemption in Ephesians 1:7; Colossians 1:14, and is the result of sacrifice in Hebrews 9:22; 10:18. Forgiveness by God accompanies his raising of sinners who were dead in trespasses (Col. 2:13; the phrase is not found in the parallel in Eph 2:6). In both Ephesians and Colossians, the readers are commanded to forgive one another as God in Christ has forgiven them (Eph. 4:32 par. Col. 3:13).

There is a remarkable omission in the actual use of the term in Paul's earlier letters. Paul tells the Corinthians to forgive the man who has been causing pain to others, including Paul himself, and states that he will share in the act (2 Cor. 2:7, 10), and there is an ironical reference in 2 Cor. 12:13 to forgiveness being extended to Paul for the fact that he had treated them worse than other churches by not being a burden to them. However, there is no reference in these earlier letters to divine forgiveness as the content of salvation.[22] Were it not for one reference found in a LXX quotation in Romans 4:7, the vocabulary of divine

---

[21] Luke 12:10 implies that forgiveness is possible for those who do not commit the unforgivable sin. Words spoken against the Son of Man will be forgiven, but not against the Holy Spirit.

[22] It can be assumed that the forgiveness extended by the congregation or its individual members includes forgiveness by God for the specific sin.

forgiveness would be completely absent from Paul's early writings.

The explanation for this omission is probably to be found in Paul's preference for the language of justification, a concept which is close in meaning to forgiveness, as Romans 4:7 makes clear. This same passage also shows that "not crediting sin to somebody" has the same force (Rom. 4:8 [LXX]; 2 Cor. 5:19; cf. 2 Tim. 4:16). This phrase is significantly also found in 2 Corinthians 5:19, thus making an important link with reconciliation; reconciliation can take place only when people's sins are not reckoned against them. Not to reckon sin is not to hold it against somebody, to regard it as if it had not happened (cf. Heb. 8:12; 10:17 citing Jer. 31:34). The sin mentioned in 2 Corinthians 5:19 corresponds to the hostility in Romans 5 and Ephesians 2; in Colossians 1, evil deeds are part of the situation that is dealt with, and the fact that the reconciled are treated as holy and unblamable suggests that the sin has been dealt with.

Forgiveness of sins is thus a concept that is particularly characteristic of Luke-Acts, but also has a strong basis in the teaching and practice of John the Baptist and Jesus.[23] It also figures in the life and teaching of the early church, according to John and 1 John. It is associated with redemption in Ephesians and Colossians, and with the effects of the sacrifice of Christ in Hebrews. The link with reconciliation is made in 2 Corinthians 5, but generally Paul prefers the language of justification.

However, that is not all. There is a rich vein of material that is best understood in this context even if the specific vocabulary is absent. Two of the parables in Luke are particularly important here.

The story of the wayward son in Luke 15:11–32 is the classic example of forgiveness and reconciliation. The situation of alienation from home, the prodigal's assumption that he could not expect a welcome back home in view of his wasteful and sinful way of life, the implicit forgiveness, the welcome back

---

[23] There is no reason to suppose that its prominent place in Acts is the product of unhistorical fancy by Luke.

not as a slave but as a son (cf. Gal. 4:7!), the lavish hospitality – all these things indicate that a reconciliatory offer is pressed upon the son.[24]

The second instance, the story of the Pharisee and the tax-collector in Luke 18:10–14, is especially interesting. Most of the other stories designated as parables describe some human happening which is to be seen as a picture of a divine-human happening or relationship. In this case, however, what we are told is a story about a divine-human happening which is then seen to be exemplary of a wider group of divine-human happenings.[25] This story is an actual example of divine-human reconciliation, not an earthly story to be interpreted in divine-human terms (in the way that the Prodigal Son is to be interpreted). A further significant point is that the tax-collector prays, "God be merciful to me the sinner," and Jesus' comment is that he goes home justified. In other words, the tax-collector experienced the answer to this prayer: God showed mercy to him, God was reconciled to him. This demonstration of mercy was an act of reconciliation. Here, then, is not a case of an apostle proclaiming the offer of reconciliation but of a sinner asking for reconciliation as if the offer was already known, or out of sheer despair because all he can do is throw himself on the mercy of God.

Even more important is the fact that the story brings together mercy,[26] justification, and reconciliation. The former two terms are actually used, while the third is crying out to be used. It is not too much to say that this story provides a vivid outworking of what is established in 2 Corinthians 5. The two passages throw light on each other. The effect of the

---

[24] Even though the son is penitent (unless we cynically assume that he is acting the part), there is no mention of faith. But he does cast himself helplessly upon the mercy of his father, and what else is faith but that?

[25] The group of similar parables includes the Good Samaritan (on the normal interpretation of it), the rich man and Lazarus, and the Great Judgement.

[26] The verb *hilaskomai* expresses the favorable attitude that the sinner implores God to show to him, and links up with the concept of Christ's death as the means by which God sacrificially expiates sins, and so demonstrates that he is propitious towards sinners who can now seek forgiveness on the basis that he has so acted (Rom. 3:25; 1 John 2:2; 4:10).

divine bearing of sin is to establish the offer of reconciliation. The death of Jesus is the means of reconciliation because, in this act, God in his mercy provides the divine equivalent for the offering of sacrifice that takes away sin and its consequences. What the Old Testament sacrifices could not really do but merely symbolized was to take away sins, i.e., to remove their guilt and the consequent liability to judgement (Heb. 10:11): this is what Christ has done. When the sinner comes to this merciful God and asks for forgiveness and reconciliation, God acts in accord with his character and on the basis of his atoning action and grants what is requested.

We have now gathered sufficient material to see the wide scope of the motif of reconciliation. The result of our survey of these related word-groups materially increases the amount of overt language regarding divine-human reconciliation and to show that the concept is widely used. The fundamental problem caused by sin is that it separates people from God and renders them liable to an attitude variously described as wrath, anger or judgement. Through the death of Jesus, God no longer reckons their sins against them; in a vivid phrase, he "slays" the enmity (Eph. 2:16), and thereby establishes the possibility of reconciliation, entailing the forgiveness of sins and establishment of peace.

A pattern exemplified

Reconciliation is only one of a number of concepts found in the Bible that refer to the process of change from a worse situation to a better. Like "salvation," "redemption," and other such terms, it presupposes a bad situation and depicts the process whereby a better one is brought about. This kind of process is the main theme in the Bible, since everywhere the sin and rebellion of humanity is a problem.[27] There is a pattern of salvation that can be widely traced in biblical teaching:

---

[27] Within the space available it is not possible to defend the existence of this pattern and to show how it finds expression in the different models of salvation.

1. The creation of a good universe by a loving and just God
2. The corruption of the universe by evil
3. The judgement of God on those who commit evil
4. The action of God in his grace to deliver the universe from its situation
5. The announcement by God of what he has done and the invitation to respond
6. The response, positive or negative, of those who hear the announcement
7. The re-creation of those who respond positively
8. The final judgement in which evil is overcome and paradise is restored

These eight points are the essential elements that form the common framework of biblical teaching, but, as I have presented them, they are extremely formal and abstract, and they leave out an enormous amount of detail and they do not express the characteristically biblical, Jewish-Christian form of the story. I have presented them in what could be regarded as a story told chronologically, but the impression that they are successive, definable stages following one after another in a historical series is manifestly an over-simplification of a much more complex set of factors. Thus, to take just one point, point four: there is not one single action of deliverance by God but many, and even the simple biblical distinction between two covenants, old and new, hides a whole set of interventions by God to restore the situation.

The concept of reconciliation can easily be seen to fit the pattern:

1. It is implicit that there was an original situation of harmony between God and the people whom he had created.[28]
2. This harmony has been disrupted, and the people display enmity (expressed in disobedience and distrust) both to God and to one another.

---

[28] This point is not greatly emphasized in the New Testament. It belongs to the distant past of Adam and Eve. It is assumed that everybody subsequent to them shares in their disobedience and rebellion.

3. God treats people as his enemies, partly now and partly in a future judgement.
4. At the same time, God acts to bring about reconciliation in the coming and death of Jesus.[29]
5. God sends his messengers to announce that forgiveness and reconciliation are offered to all who will accept his offer and return to him.
6. People either respond with faith and are reconciled or they reject the message and remain as enemies of God.
7. God's purpose for his people begins to be fulfilled in the establishment of his peaceable community (the kingdom or church) where people love and serve God and one another.
8. God will finally reject those who refuse to be reconciled, and his purpose for his reconciled people will be fully realized.

Other models of salvation

Against this background I now want to look at the other models of salvation that are used in the New Testament, especially by Paul, to see how they relate to reconciliation. Ideally, we should consider them in as much detail as we have devoted to reconciliation, but here we can do no more than summarize the main points that characterize them, so that we may place them alongside reconciliation. My purpose is to show that these are similar in structure to the motif of reconciliation and often closely linked with it, but that reconciliation may well be the most comprehensive and the most apt of the models that are used.

There are three types of model to be discussed: first, models that cover both the process involved in the work of Christ and the resulting situation for believers; second, a model for the work of Christ itself; and, third, models for the effects of the work of Christ without direct reference as to how these are achieved.

---

[29] I pass over all the attempts to create an obedient people in the Old Testament story.

The work of Christ and the resulting benefits

Justification

First, we look at models for the work of Christ and its results, beginning with justification. The discussion of justification is complicated by the way in which scholars postulate different types of background for the concept: judicial, forensic, or cosmic. While the vocabulary, as a whole, can have a broader usage than the judicial process, the New Testament usage of the verb "justify" seems to me to be best understood against a legal background. The action is that of a judge; evil is understood as transgression of the law; and justification itself is an act of acquittal that is paradoxically the acquittal of the guilty on the basis of Christ's death and resurrection, and identification with him by faith.

In Paul, the concept is developed in Galatians and Romans, where he is dealing with the problem of the salvation of Gentiles, and his solution is that justification is by faith alone, alike for Jews and Gentiles. Justification turns out to be the most appropriate vehicle for understanding how Gentiles may be saved, and its centrality is related to two facts. One is the use of "righteousness" in relation to the place of Abraham; the other is the fact that the debate over the place of Gentiles in the Christian community and their relationship to Jewish believers, had been conducted in terms of the law and the works required by it.

Although the essential points in our eightfold summary of the pattern of salvation can be traced in Paul's use of the concept, nevertheless justification has its limitations as a model. It is essentially confined to Paul and his followers. Some aspects of salvation are less prominent here – I do not say totally absent – such as deliverance from the power of sin, the implementation of a new life, and the social dimension. This reminds us that no one model of God's saving action and the resulting salvation was ever regarded as adequate to embrace every aspect of the matter. Paul is certainly conscious of this fact, particularly in the light of possible Jewish objections to his doctrine. He faces up to them squarely in Romans 6–8. In these chapters, he sets justification in a broader context of union with Christ and empowerment by the Spirit through which the believer is released by death with Christ from the dominion of sin and raised to a new life in the Spirit. Although justification is concerned with the individual sinner, in Romans 5, Paul discusses the corporate nature of both sin and justification, and he shows how Jews and Gentiles are both saved in the same way and thus form one people of God.

Justification is the process whereby sinners are "put right" with God, and it can be seen as one way of expressing how reconciliation is brought about between God and human beings. It focuses on the role of God as judge, but, in placing it within the context of reconciliation, it indicates that, while God does not abandon his judicial role as the upholder of righteousness, nevertheless the forgiveness and new status of the justified leads into a situation of peace with a God who is their Father.

Redemption
The underlying metaphor in redemption is that of slavery to the hostile powers or to sin; redemption is deliverance from the mastery of sin and from the wages paid by sin, namely death. The result of redemption is, at one level, the transfer of slaves to a new master. Even on this level a personal element is present in that redemption includes the transfer of ownership of the former sinner to a new master. However, in Galatians and Romans, the model is transcended. The effect of redemption is adoption as children in a way that must include but transcend slavery. That is to say, the thought of obedience is still there, but it is rendered to a Father rather than to a slave master.

The metaphor broadens out in Romans 8:23, where adoption and the redemption of the body are linked. Hebrews 9:15, in effect, makes the redemption of sinners from former sins equivalent to their forgiveness.

Although there is a background in the Old Testament of redemption being carried out by a kinsman, this element is not so explicit in the NT, and the personal term "redeemer" was not developed to any extent as a title or description for God or Christ.

Redemption as a model has less to say about relationship to God and forgiveness, but emphasizes the setting free of the sinner from the power of sin and from its consequences. Here the consequence of sin, namely death, is understood more in terms of what sin does to its victims rather than as a sentence carried out by God (for which cf. Rom. 1:32). Redemption thus makes up for the lack of emphasis in the reconciliation model of deliverance from the power of sin and the hostile forces opposed to God.

As with justification, the social, corporate element is not stressed.

Salvation

Salvation is a term closely akin in meaning to redemption.[30] It became the concept that is probably most used in Christian theology and preaching to refer to the results of the work of Christ and gave rise to the title of Savior, whereas the title of Redeemer was, perhaps surprisingly, not developed. In salvation the two metaphors of healing and rescue combine. The former conveys the idea of the human plight as a form of illness, an illness that can be fatal. The latter can convey the idea of deliverance from danger.

The danger is the judgement of God upon sin, and hence salvation is closely linked with justification as it refers primarily to deliverance from the judgement of God. Paul does, on occasion, use it with a focus on the future experience of deliverance from God's wrath and the resultant destruction at the final judgement. But this is only one usage, and the term can equally be used for a present deliverance. To speak of God or Christ as Savior purely in respect of an awaited future deliverance is unrealistic. The use of present and past tenses is natural (Rom. 8:24; 1 Cor. 1:18, 21; 15:2; Eph. 2:5, 8; 2 Tim. 1:9; Titus 3:5; 1 Pet. 3:21).

---

[30] Marshall, I. H. "Salvation." In *New Dictionary of Theology*, edited by S. B. Ferguson and D. F. Wright. Leicester: IVP, 1988, 610–611.

In this perspective, salvation could be understood in a negative sense. But it also serves as an all-encompassing positive term, like peace, to convey the totality of God's blessings bestowed on believers (Luke 19:9; Rom. 1;16). It implicitly brings out the fact of deliverance by someone other than themselves, rescue for those who cannot rescue themselves, salvation brought about by a Savior.

Salvation is thus a broad concept that could include the others. But the picture can also be reduced to a description of a process that could be understood somewhat impersonally on the analogies of healing and rescue. As with some of the other models, the social dimension is not to the fore. Nevertheless, it complements reconciliation by its recognition that there is more to the process than simply the canceling out of the past sin; there is a process of healing.

The work of Christ itself

Sacrifice

These four terms – reconciliation, justification, redemption and salvation – all have a similar grammar in that they refer to an action of God and the resulting state of those who believe. Believers are reconciled, justified, redeemed and saved; they are in the words of a hymn "ransomed, healed, restored, forgiven." These adjectives describe what God has achieved. A different type of term is sacrifice, which is used to describe what Christ has done, rather than what he has achieved; it expresses what he has done in order to achieve what is expressed by these other terms.

The model is drawn from typical ancient religious ritual. Although not all sacrifices functioned in the same way, the sacrifice was primarily a means of achieving or expressing a positive relationship with God through a costly offering. The way in which sacrifice functioned is debated, and it is probable that we should combine the three elements of gift, communion, and atonement which have been variously thought to lie at the origins of Hebrew practice. In the Old Testament, the sacrificial system is instituted by God, who has laid down the ways in which sacrifice is to be offered.

Hence the system can be regarded as his gracious provision of a means of atonement and communion with himself.

The result of the sacrifices for sin was that the sin no longer stood against the sinner; the sinner is no longer liable to judgement.[31] But, whereas the terms so far considered can be used to describe the state of those on whose behalf something has been done, the term sacrifice does not lead to the creation of a cognate term for the people whose sins have been atoned for. For this state we have to use the terminology taken from the models already discussed.

Another solution is to follow the example of Hebrews which uses the language of holiness and sanctification. This gives us the process-term "sanctification" and the state-term "sanctity" or "holiness." We then have a concept of a people originally being or intended to be holy (a word that includes moral behavior) and failing to be so. God intervenes by providing a sacrifice which has the effect of undoing the mess and bringing the people to a state of holiness.

The process is a wide one in that it is concerned not just with the holiness of individuals, but also with the holiness of the people as a nation and of the land in which they live. Nevertheless, it must be remembered that sacrificial language is also used in contexts other than sanctification, for example, in Romans 3, it is used in close connection with justification.

The model of sacrifice is thus sharply focused on the way in which the death and exaltation of Jesus are to be understood. It is taken from the major biblical tradition in which the broken relationship between sinners and God is restored. It is used in connection with reconciliation and justification to indicate how they take place.

The benefits of Christ's work

The family
A third type of language is concerned with models or pictures that describe the result of God's action without

---

[31] The effect of sacrifice is also to cleanse the land from the pollution caused by the sin of its people.

reference to the action itself. An important concept is that of the family. The picture of God as Father and human beings as his children could be used to describe the state that has been perverted. It is not used of the situation of Gentiles; the concept of humanity in general as the children of God by creation may be found outside the Bible, but, within it, it is the nation of Israel which is the "son" of God, and gradually this relationship came to be used of godly individuals. In the parabolic imagery used by Jesus, the figure of the son can be used for the son who goes away from home and needs to be brought back and restored to his former position. (Luke 15:11–32; cf. Matt. 21:28–32; it would be risky to argue from this parable that Gentiles, as well as tax-collectors and prostitutes, are to be understood as "sons" who have gone astray). However, the result of the saving action is the granting of the new status of sons and daughters (or children) to those who formerly were outside the family or who were slaves. The blessings can then be expounded in terms of the inheritance granted to children.

As we have previously noted, the roles of father and judge can be combined in view of the ancient concept of fatherhood (1 Pet. 1:17). This goes beyond the concept of the father as simply exercising discipline over the members of the family (Heb. 12:4–11).

Implicit here is the relationship of believers to one another as brothers (a term that includes sisters), a common term for referring to this relationship, but figures only marginally in theological discussion of salvation. It is used of relationship to Christ (Rom. 8:29; Heb. 2:11) and in appeals for brotherly love (Rom. 14:10–21; 1 Cor. 6:5–8; 8:11–13; 1 Thess. 4:6; Phlm. 16; espec. 1 John 2:9–11; 3:10–18; 4:20–21; 5:16).

However, this motif says very little about the actual process of adoption and the place of Christ in that process. Its importance is that it expresses most fully the nature of the new relationship that results from the act of reconciliation.

The covenant
Alongside the family concept we should also note that of the covenant, with its background in the Old Testament teaching

about a new covenant that replaces the old one. This new covenant is established by the death of Jesus, and is now enlarged to include the Gentiles. The imagery is used more in a corporate sense of the relationship of the people as a whole to God, but, in the end, this comes down to the relationship of individuals to him. In this context, the thought of family break-up might arise, as in references in the Old Testament to God's wayward children, but it does not seem to be part of the picture in the New Testament. The thought of covenant-breaking as leading to exile, a judgement that involves some kind of separation from God, may be brought in at this point, and some scholars have argued that this is a significant underlying element in the New Testament. The idea that the covenant is inaugurated or restored by sacrifice is an integral part of the picture, probably with the thought that the sacrifice cleanses and dedicates those who take part in it.

The covenant motif is used to bring out the relationship of the Christ-event and the people of God to the history of God's earlier dealings with Israel. It is thus of fundamental structural importance in the exposition of salvation history, but, otherwise, its role is not as apparent as might have been expected (with the notable exception of its place in Hebrews). It figures in a reconciliation context in Ephesians 2:12, where it serves the important function of showing how the reconciliation offered in and through Christ brings rebellious Jews and distant Gentiles into the one people of God. The related concept of mediation is a further link between the two concepts.

A comparison of models

We have now considered three types of concept or language used to describe what Christ does and its results. Each of the descriptions of the process fits the formal pattern that I found to be exemplified in reconciliation to greater or less extent. Human need, divine provision in the work of Christ, and a resulting transformation of the situation are the three basic elements.

The fact that so many different pictures are used in the New Testament suggests that no single one is adequate to convey the whole story. Some features stand out more clearly in some documents than in others. This warns us against expecting any single picture to be comprehensive. What we have in the NT is a mixture of overlapping pictures and stories that express this basic pattern in different ways. I suspect that the overlap is such that if any one of the distinguishable threads was deleted, its absence would be well covered by the others.

There are inter-links between the pictures. They are not sharply differentiated from one another, but run into each other. This is particularly clear in Romans 5 where justification and reconciliation are used side by side as alternative ways of expressing the same reality; both are the present experiences that guarantee future salvation. We have noted that the New Testament conception of a father included his activity akin to that of a judge exercised over the members of the family. The New Testament speaks of God as Father far more often than as judge, but the model of justification brings out the judicial aspect of his character and activity in a way that might otherwise be overlooked. The models thus meld into one another. (Nevertheless, the term that came to be characteristically used for God is "Father," not "judge," and we pray to "our Father in heaven," not to "our judge in heaven."[32])

Within this complex, therefore, it may be wrong to expect one particular picture to sum up the thought adequately. Even the concept of reconciliation does not explicitly contain every element of the total picture. We have seen how it lacks the language of guilt in the sense of breaking laws, but arguably this element is covered by the references to rebellion and enmity. Likewise, the language of divine judgement is replaced by the thought of God treating his enemies in appropriate ways. It also lacks the concept of

---

[32] Whilst there are many uses of "father" as a description or title for God in the New Testament, we find "judge" used only in Acts 10:42 (of Christ); 2 Timothy 4:8; Hebrews 12:23; James 4:12; 5:9. There are, of course, many more references to divine judgement.

slavery to sin from which one cannot get free by one's own efforts. Although, it recognizes that the death of Jesus brings the enmity to an end, it does not explain fully how this happens. Nor does this model bring out the "family" element of becoming sons and daughters of God. However, it has close links with justification, and the resultant, continuing harmony (Rom. 5:1).

Nevertheless, there is a strong case that the concept of reconciliation (including peace and forgiveness) is pretty comprehensive, that the motif is widespread, and that the rationale underlies both Pauline thought in particular, and New Testament thought generally. The positive elements in the concept of reconciliation seem to me to outweigh the elements that may be thought to be lacking, and I do not think that a better case can be made for any of the other models.

We may note four important positive factors brought out especially by the motif of reconciliation.

First, reconciliation particularly brings out the fact that the basic problem is the breakdown or lack of a positive personal relationship between sinners and God. A narrow view of redemption sees the problem as captivity to sin rather than as a broken relationship with God. The family and covenant pictures are more personal. Justification is concerned with a more legal type of relationship, although we should not play the one against the other. Salvation is similar to redemption. The picture of sacrifice also deals with a broken relationship due to sin, and expresses a principle that is common to all the pictures of how that relationship is restored. Salvation is essentially the repair of a broken relationship with God, and the process of doing this is aptly summed up and expressed in reconciliation.

Second, R. Bultmann commented:

One might almost say that in using the term "reconciliation" Paul's intention to show man's radical dependence upon the grace of God is still more clearly expressed than when he uses the term "righteousness of God," for while the latter means that *without* our doing anything we arrive at "peace" with

God (Rom. 5:1), the former means that *before* any effort of man God made an end of enmity (Rom. 5:10). But in substance, of course, there is no difference: both "without us" and "before us" intend to declare the absolute priority of God.[33]

It is not the case that the other models do not express this priority. The sacrificial system, for example, is presented as God's provision for sinners, and the covenant is pre-eminently the offer made by a suzerain to an inferior group. Nevertheless, reconciliation does bring out poignantly the role of God himself. In reconciliation, the initiative lies with God himself, the mediator is God in the person of God the Son, the reconciliation is brought about by God entering into the plight of sinners and enduring the consequences of their sin,[34] and then sending his messengers to call rebels to repentance and faith. Again, the language is that of personal relationships, broken by sin, and now restored by God.

Third, reconciliation brings the sinner into a restored relationship with God. It thus expresses directly the nature of salvation in both its positive and its negative senses. At the heart of the Christian religion is the mutual relationship of love between the Father and his children. This goes beyond the cancellation of guilt and even the imputation of righteousness that is at the heart of justification. Certainly, the somewhat negative impression that some people receive from the term justification, thinking of it solely in terms of canceling out of past sin, is one-sided, since the term includes the conferral of a positive righteous status. The combination of "reconciliation" and "peace" indicates rather more positively the new situation of those who are reconciled.

In the light of these considerations, the claim that reconciliation is particularly well-suited to bring out the heart of the work of Christ and the new situation that it brings into being stands. Although reconciliation is not widely thematic in the

---

[33] Bultmann, *Theology*, I, 287; cited by Stuhlmacher, *Theologie* I, 337.

[34] This is effected by the substitutionary death of Christ, bearing the rebelliousness and sin of God's enemies, and suffering the exclusion from God which is the penalty that would otherwise befall those who do not want to live under God as their Lord.

New Testament, nevertheless, it does provide the organizing principle, the underlying concept, that enables us to perceive some unity and harmony in the range of other models and motifs used to describe the salvation of God and the way in which he effects it.

The social implications of reconciliation

There is a further, distinctive, aspect of reconciliation that demands to be highlighted by giving it separate treatment. It might be thought that one element lacking in the model is the transformation of the reconciled into a new people. But this is, in fact, present in the way that reconciliation makes the social dimension of salvation more explicit than do some of the other pictures (specifically redemption, salvation, justification).

The risk with using any of these pictures is that they can be understood individualistically of the relationship of the single person to God. Indeed, to digress, much of our worship has historically turned a congregation into a set of isolated individuals each in vertical, personal relationship to God. It is a welcome sign of change that the sideways, or horizontal, relationship has begun to be expressed in contexts where there is a formal sharing of peace with one another or where each of us receives the bread and the cup from our brother/sister in Christ and then passes them on to our brother/sister in Christ. Ultimately religion is a matter of my personal, individual response to Christ, a response that only I can make,[35] but this response involves also a two-way relationship to my Christian brothers and sisters.

How does this work out in reconciliation with God?

Paul argues that Jews and Gentiles are united in sin, all being in Adam; similarly, they can be united in salvation, all being united with Christ and becoming one as children of Abraham, having faith in God and being credited with

---

[35] I except, of course, those situations where I am unable to do so and others pray to God for me.

righteousness. The difference between those who are physical descendants of Abraham and those who are his spiritual descendants is of no significance as the crucial factor is that both are justified by faith.

The great advantage of the term "reconciled" is that it can be used equally aptly of the divine-human and the human-human relationships, whereas the term "justified" cannot be used of the latter; the same point applies to much of the other language that is used.

The ways in which this human reconciliation must be expressed are various. On one hand, there is the important argument that those who are forgiven by God must forgive one another (Matt. 6:12–15; 18:21–35; Mark 11:25; Luke 11:4; Eph. 4:32; Col. 3:13). On the other hand, there is the command to love one another as God has loved us (John 13:34; 15:12; Eph. 5:1–2, 25; 1 John 4:11–12, 19). This is fortified by the Johannine teaching that love for one another is an essential component of our love for God, so much so, that lack of the former is visible evidence of lack of the latter (1 John 4:20).[36]

It is taken for granted that the expected behavior of brothers and sisters is that they live together in love and unity (Ps. 133:1[37]). Certainly this is an ideal which may not always be realized (the rot set in with Cain and Abel and extends to the community addressed in 1 John). Quarrels between brothers and sisters are particularly odious. Consequently, the fact that people are constituted as brothers and sisters in the family of God carries the clear implication that there should be a relationship of unity between them. This love is based on the fact that those who love a father will love his children (1 John 5:1–2)

In Ephesians 2, Paul uses the doctrine of reconciliation to express this point of the unity of believing Jews and Gentiles. The underlying assumption is that the separation of the

---

[36] Cf. Romans 15:7 where the thought is expressed in terms of welcoming one another.

[37] The point is lost in translations (such as TNIV) which translate with "God's people"; NRSV "kindred" is better, since the reference of the Hebrew *'aḥîm* is broader than just to "brothers."

Gentiles was not only from God but also from his people who stood in relationship to God; the Gentiles have now been brought near to God and made part of his people. The means by which peace brought about by God includes a specific peace-making between Jews and Gentiles. This is stated as an objective fact; God himself has removed any possible grounds for difference between them. The incorporation of Gentiles in Christ is incorporation in Israel. This is possible because the law has been set aside and no longer condemns them. At the same time it is clear that Paul is speaking of the new Israel (regardless of whether he uses that term), in which the Jews are also members on the same basis of faith as the Gentiles, not by works of the law but by possession of the same Spirit. The readers, therefore, can and must instantiate the peace that objectively exists. Similar arguments are used elsewhere, especially in Galatians and Romans, to insist that Jews and Gentiles are reconciled and justified on the same terms as one another and that there is now one people of God composed of believing Jews and Gentiles.

In Ephesians, Paul is thus concerned especially with the place of the Gentiles in the church; their reconciliation to God and their incorporation in his people are the two essential facets of the one event. This point is not so explicit in Colossians. There the focus is more on the salvation of the Gentiles as the marvelous new revelation turned into a reality through Christ. It is the universal scope of the headship of Christ that is the issue; the relationship of Jews and Gentiles in the church is not such a basic issue. Nevertheless, it is stressed that earthly distinctions are irrelevant where Christ is at the heart of communal life, and the members of his body must live at peace (Col. 3:11–15).

Moving backwards, we come to Romans. Here the concept of reconciliation is introduced primarily to indicate how the present situation of peace with God is the ground for a sure hope of deliverance from the wrath of God at the last judgement. But the practical lesson is drawn: "accept one another, just as Christ has accepted you" (Rom. 15:7).

Similarly, in 2 Corinthians 5–6 the primary focus is again on the personal relationship with God. The language used sounds distinctly evangelistic. Yet, it becomes the basis for an appeal to the readers to be welcoming to Paul. A congregation that claims to be at peace with God should also be at peace with the missionaries who act as his representatives. It is the lack of openness and affection of the Corinthians to Paul that is the issue (2 Cor. 6:12–13). This would be a more limited expression, but at the same time a very practical and important corollary of reconciliation.

Where the language is evangelistic, however, its use carries the implication that those who make known the gospel and who live as Christians in the world share the reconciling love of the God whose servants they are. They cannot very well preach a gospel of reconciliation to a people with whom they themselves are not prepared to live in peace and love. One cannot shout the gospel across a chasm to people on the other side so that they may have a relationship with God above but not one with those on this side of the chasm.

Here is the foundation for a Christian attitude of love and reconciliation to all people. We reach out in love to all humankind because all are the objects of a love that does not want any to perish but all to come to a knowledge of the truth and respond positively to the gospel. This love of God's is not dependent upon anyone's response but is offered to all, even to those who continue to reject it. Whether those who reject this love will ultimately be rejected by God is his concern, not ours. For the time being, it remains true that "now is the time of God's favor, now is the day of salvation" (2 Cor. 6:2), and it is not within our jurisdiction to declare that this time is over.

It is not surprising, then, that there are frequent injunctions to believers to be peace-makers, and reminders that one of the effects of the Spirit who dwells in them is to bring about peace. That this is not merely an interior peace of mind is clear from the company that the term keeps with words that convey ethical attitudes to other people (Rom. 14:17–19; 1 Cor. 7:15; Eph. 4:3; Col. 3:15; 2 Tim. 2:22; Heb. 12:14; Jas. 3:17–18; 1 Pet. 3:11).

My contention is that the nature of reconciliation brings out this aspect of salvation more explicitly and directly than other images.[38] This is not to deny that this aspect of Christian behavior is implied in the other descriptions. We have seen that justification is closely linked to the new life in Christ, a life of righteousness in which the law is fulfilled by living in love. Redemption sets us free from the power of sin in order to do good works. Salvation is understood in the same kind of way. The creation of a holy people likewise emphasizes new living; thus in 1 Thessalonians 4 the rather negative description of holiness as the avoidance of lust and greed is immediately followed by the positive commendation of love for one another. But the teaching that we have seen to be bound up with the broad concept of reconciliation, forgiveness and peace expresses the call for loving human relationships all the more powerfully and firmly grounds human behavior in the way that God treats us. In particular, the recognition that the gift of salvation requires willingness to forgive as God has forgiven us comes out most powerfully in the concept of reconciliation.

One problem remains. This New Testament call for reconciliation with all people does not seem to provide a basis for reconciliation between peoples who do not share the theological, christological and indeed pneumatological[39] foundation of its appeal. It roots reconciliation in the purpose of God to restore his original intention for creation through re-creation. It also sees the barriers to reconciliation as lying in the sinfulness of humanity from which they need to be saved. The New Testament appeal is addressed to the people who are reconciled with God to see that this reconciliation carries with it the inescapable obligation to offer the same reconciliation to other people and to live as peace-makers. It is primarily concerned that believers should set their own house in order by living according to the way of life laid down for them by their God. But how does this affect reconciliation with and between people of other religious faiths and none?

---

[38] The family model could be in danger of envisaging a love that is purely "within the family."

[39] Romans 14:17; Ephesians 4:3.

Of course, it is the case that many people accept the Christian ethic as a desirable ideal to which they ought to strive. Many other religious people also stress peace and reconciliation as desirable goals, and so also do many humanists. Therefore, there is hope of some progress towards peace and reconciliation even where the Christian faith is not accepted. And we must regretfully acknowledge that this will for reconciliation on the part of some non-Christians is balanced by the retaliatory and hostile attitudes adopted in both the past and present by some professing Christians. We, as Christians, need to express sorrow over the evil that has been done by those who profess to be Christian, and to speak out, as the prophets did, against continuing evil of the same kind.

It is also appropriate for us to commend the contribution that acceptance of the Christian way can make to peace and reconciliation. To use a comparable situation: there is no doubt that the initial spread of AIDS and much of its continuing spread has been due to a sexual promiscuity that is forbidden by a Christian sexual ethic. Stopping the spread of the disease would be greatly (even though not completely) facilitated by adoption of Christian teaching and practice. Nevertheless, this does not mean that progress towards curbing it cannot and should not be made by other means, such as so-called "safe sex." As Christians, we have a duty to proclaim our gospel and our ethic as the right and best way for humanity, but this does not mean that we refuse to recognize the value of other approaches that have some positive effect.

So too a commendation of the Christian rejection of seeking revenge and achieving political ends by violence is appropriate in the world of today. To be sure, Christians cannot rest content with a human society that leaves out a personal relationship with the God and Father of the Lord Jesus Christ, and we may well believe that ultimately those who are motivated and empowered through their own reconciliation with God are the ones best placed to bring about reconciliation in human society, but this does not mean that we deny or ignore the efforts at reconciliation that are motivated in other ways.

The Christian doctrine is realistic in its recognition that the fundamental cause of disharmony lies in human sinfulness and rejection of God's law of love. It is through a common acceptance of God's ways that reconciliation comes about between warring human beings. We can rejoice that recognition of the need for living by justice and love is not peculiar to Christians, while, at the same time, maintaining that the fullest manifestation of such living is possible only where people are motivated by love for the God who first loved them and reconciled them to himself and are empowered by the Spirit of peace whom God bestows upon them.

Conclusion

I would claim, then, that our enquiry has demonstrated that reconciliation is a model that expresses clearly the basic pattern of human need, God's action, and the resultant new situation that shapes all the biblical imagery of salvation, and that it does so in a way that is particularly comprehensive and is especially relevant in a world where the need for new relationships between human beings is so clamant.

Index of Authors

ND - #0119 - 270225 - C0 - 216/140/8 - PB - 9781842275498 - Gloss Lamination